Niagara Lost and Found

New and Selected Poems

E.R. Baxter III

Abyss Publications
Yarmouthport, MA

Baxter's distinctive poetry has entertained us over the years–with its vivid images, insights, and sometimes amusing lines, which celebrate place and the fleeting moment, those observations about living that we all treasure. His writing about Niagara, a natural phenomenon about which torrents of words have continued to flow for centuries, is characterized by a soaring lyricism that is unequalled. He was witness to the mimeo revolution, indeed, was part of it, and many of his early publications are kept by the Poetry Collection of the University Libraries, University at Buffalo, State University of New York.

There you may see the out-of-print *Looking for Niagara* (which the late Hugh Fox called "a book with a wallop"), and also *What I Want*, along with the chapbook *Hunger*, and the slim book entitled (as he pokes gentle fun at himself) *And Other Poems*. He also had work in the now collectable *Peace Amongst the Ants;* had easelwork in the First Annual Concrete Poetry Exhibition in Vancouver, BC (late 60's); and received a Best of Experimental Work award (concrete poetry) from Gene Bloom's *Entrails* magazine (1969).

We at Abyss are pleased to bring you *Niagara Lost and Found: New and Selected Poems*–which includes a broad range of Niagara poetry, the entire text of *What I Want*, and new poems, as well, including "Finding Niagara," the completion of the Niagara cycle, and the long and powerful poem "God."

***

The final poet to read this evening is E.R. Baxter III. This is appropriate because the book being celebrated here is about the River, herself, and so for this position I could only think of Bob. Yes, he is an English professor and the author of numerous pieces, including his latest, *Niagara Digressions*. But there is so much more to him.

In fact, I will tell you something about the Bob I know. This man has stopped by the library looking for a razor blade–instead of a book. He isn't playing games here. His world and words are raw and fresh. They will bleed all over you.

And I can promise you that if you give him time, he will ruffle your feathers. He will make you uncomfortable. He is an activist and has spent much of his life fighting for the integrity of Niagara. He is passionate in his beliefs and he is fearless. Sometimes he is alone.

But he knows Niagara well. And he prefers her wild and unkempt, unharnessed and free. Actually, I think he's a lot like Niagara.

So listen to his poetry and read his words. It won't be long before you understand Niagara, too.

Michelle Kratts, Librarian
Lewiston Public Library
Lewiston, NY

Acknowledgements:

Some poems in this book have been previously published by: Abyss Publications; Black Rabbit Press; *Earth's Daughters: A Feminist Arts Periodical; The Little Mag*; Lone Ranger Biology Press; *Lost Creek Letters; Pyramid; Slipstream Magazine;* Slipstream Publications; *Trace; and Wormwood Review*.

Grateful appreciation and credits to: Harry Brashear for the barbershop and the cover photographs; to Larry Coleman for the cover design; to Richard Piza for the spray paint art of the back cover; and to Jeremy Smith for electronic manuscript preparation.

A special thank you to Eric Gansworth for the selection of poems that appear in this book, and for creating the format in which they are presented.

"The Reason for Skylarks" By Kenneth Patchen. from COLLECTED POEMS OF KENNETH PATCHEN, copyright (c) 1954 by New Directions Publishing Corp. Reprinted by permission of New Directions Publishing Corp.

For permission to reproduce the oil painting on the cover, thank you to Michelle Petrazzoulo, the Executive Director of the Earl Brydges Library, Niagara Falls,

New York, where the painting is on display, and to Linda Reinumagi of the library's Local History for helping to narrow the choice to this image of the American Falls.

The painting, entitled The Rock of Ages, was completed in 1896, by artist George W. King (1838-1922). The canvas is 4', 5 ½" wide, and 5', 7" high, mounted in an ornate, gilded frame, 8 ½" wide. The following appeared in the Niagara Gazette on 5 September 1896:

"It is truly a noble picture and is destined to become famous...The view presented is grand and looks from Fisherman's Rock from the shore of Goat Island in the gorge up across the Center and American Falls. In the foreground the Rock of Ages stands prominently forth. The accuracy of the artist's conception of his subject is best portrayed in the spray laden atmosphere so natural to the locality, but which so very few artists...show in their work. The color of the water at different points is very natural. The rising spray is easily distinguished from the hovering clouds and affords further evidence of a master hand having held the brush."

ISBN: 978-0-911856-02-6
Library of Congress Cataloging Number: 2013903670

Abyss Publications
32 Bray Farm Road North
Yarmouthport, MA 02675-1550
AbyssPublications@gmail.com

Table of Contents

Part One: Looking for Niagara

MIST

Seven miles long
is Niagara gorge
and some nights
the mist from
the falls creeps
in it deep down
in mingling with
the fog, swelling
full-bodied
in the gorge
and extending
cautious tendrils
up into the city

"Just gorge fog,"
folks say
as the city fills
in like undersea,
the buildings fade
and streetlights are
dim beacons holding
the city to an uneasy
geometric existence

As one night mists
rise up heavy
and thick, even
the streetlights
will wink out

like snuffed candles

and when the fog
lifts in the morning
the whole city
will be gone.

NIGHT GAME

Some late night when
you do not sleep, pull

an image of distant city
out of mind, dial Information

and ask that tired voice
of authority for the number

of a person there
who bears your name. Ask
for yourself. Connections

are made, electrical impulses
racing over the cool country,

single line, zig-zag
through the tangle of bright
interchanges, piercing, according

to directive, into the web
of your desire. The auditory
canal extends across the continent,

a voice from far off,
speaking in another year,
informs you that you are not there.

Thank you. The line

dies. It is an experience
that has cost little.

Think the distances,
the sleepless and sleeping people
whose names you do not know.

ROBINS DO NOT COME TO 3rd STREET, but it is easy to tell when it is spring

From the hotplate cubicle
of second floor room the first
old man has appeared

in the street, dragging the lint
and stain of winter confinement
with him. Hat with brim down

all the way around, drab
overcoat buttoned up to neck,
he stands back to brick wall,
washed in pale sunlight, considering

relocation, demolition, redevelopment.
"Re-new-all" he pronounces it. It feels
like a vague fear to his tongue.

What the hell, he says
to himself, I've weathered
worse, I'll weather this.
He unbuttons his overcoat,
lets it hang open in the still
cold air, bravely exposing
a faded red sweater which
he casually does not
unbutton.

Thin-lidded eyes half closed against
the bright day, skin drawn tight
over beak nose, his head turns slowly
on its corded neck, his weak eyes
peering at the familiar street
as if seeing it the first time.

He thinks of moving, of the buildings
being razed, the open space that will
remain, the ground-brick littered, the butt
ends left. Would weeds grow, wildflowers–then
would robins come? It is too much to answer.

In what direction
the sea. He wades off into
the flow of the street, a dog drifts
by his knees, children caught in
games of tag swirl past, his steps

arc careful, as if under the softness
of his clothing his body might break
as if undercurrents might sweep him
off his feet into the gutter. He eases

with uncertain balance off curbs, creeps
across the street in front of waiting cars
and teeters up onto far sidewalks–

His measured going plumbs the city blocks.
From doorway to doorway the colors and noises

change. One following the other, the bars
and souvenir shops and department stores
drift into his vision
and out again.

He does not pause to look back.
His feeble forward motion cannot contend
with what is past. He does not concern himself
with what lies ahead, beyond that revealed
by eyes, "not what they
usta be."

The end of the street swims in his
spectacles. There the old men gather
in the park, and there, day after day
he joins them.

They hold quiet council with one another:
the war, the moonshots, hippies, short skirts.
Finally, they blink and nod in the warm sunshine,
while summer roars by on its windy feet.

WINTER, AND THE OLD MEN
IN THE PUBLIC LIBRARY ON MAIN

It is not
like it has been. There are

the so easily slipped
into eddies and back washes

Winter lies again
white in the streets
and across the land

the old men take daily refuge
from the cold in public libraries

each old man
a shadow of himself

detached from the shadows
of the City Mission, walking

the unerring walk
of the aged to the Public Library,

removing the overshoes just inside
the door, sitting himself

at reading tables
near the radiators. There are

the daily newspapers
waiting to be read from
the first page to the last

carefully, the comic pages
and the society news considered
with as much care as headlines.

The translucent
fingers move to the mouth
picking up just enough dampness

singularly, the pages
are evenly turned,
floating neatly down on
the pages read before them
and so, until the newspapers are read.

Outside
it is snowing

and inside
in the uneven breathing
of the blind radiators, the old sorrows

resurrect themselves. That the days
and nights are so long, that there

is so much time

for regret. Even the old

newspapers, now consigned to green
microfilm, can no longer be read
as once they could

the fragile and faded pages
turned, reading

Pearl Harbor again
and Normandy Invasion, and once

seeing a friend's name
in an obituary column.

It was as if he did not die
in the year of the old paper

but only then, decades later
as his name was read.

The flesh of memory
becomes the dust of the present

and the essence of the man
is transformed into tiny
black bones of alphabet
neatly arranged in a news-

paper column, born

died, name caught up
in a backwash of old newsprint
fading before our eyes, OBITUARY

NOTICES, and even this gone
given up to slick microfilm.

The old man turns
to the stacks of magazines,
discontentedly leafing
through their bright pages–

he looks at *Argosy*
at *Home and Garden*
at *Fortune*, at *Time*
he looks at *Life*, turning
its colorful pages, periodically
glancing through the window
at murder in the cold streets.

Note: This poem refers to the old Carnegie Library, Main Street,
Niagara Falls, NY, no longer a library, now listed on the National
Historical Register.

MY BABY LOVES THEM OLD-TIME MOVIES

1.

where
was it, the Bellevue,
Strand, the Cataract?
when you first
took my hand
his face
filling the screen
hair brilliantined
mustache pencil thin
and her face
soft, out
of focus
closeup kiss

spare
me, spare me
let us not hold
hands in the balcony
and where
is it this
time? the Amendola,
the Rainbo?
the movie
is a love
story, your

palm is moist
it is too much

the usher looking
on, leer behind
the stab of his
flashlight beam.

2.

your hand is
curled in mine
dim in the late TV
the sound
turned down

Niagara falling
silently over
the screen

I'm remembering
elephants screaming,
Johnny Weissmuller
come down
a vine
to Jungle
Jim huffing
and puffing
through undergrowth
fighting clogged

arteries, thoughts
of Jane
keeping company
with a member
of the A.N.C.
Cheetah's big
hand in front
of toothy smile

you are sleeping
fingers twitching
in the flickering
light, tiny
ghosts held
in the hand.

3.

clap hands, clap
hands, we all
fall down

somewhere
beneath the flesh
near the slim bones
of your hand
memory gleams

it lies close
to the blood warmed

by the clapping

look, look, shine
a flashlight through.

APOLOGY TO THE MOON
AND OTHER THINGS

The moon,
silver and remote,
hangs out of my reach,
so I give you this place

in chunks, in slivers,
hoping that in the end they
will come together, of a piece.

Cartographers record earth's lovely poem
lines of landscape flowing, river, lake:
an unfolded map, smoothed flat,
flooded by the sunlight of the lamp

while high above the desk and house
the naked moon rides prey to voyeuristic
telescopes, not so much up there, as out there,
where Winter Wonderlands and postcards are
of no consequence. But to be sure

of where we're at,
and before we get ahead,
should put a finger to the thing
and look with a lover's hot eyes:

On the map two lines compress
a river's width: the Niagara,

according to the legend
about thirty-six miles long,
flowing from Erie, dividing
around the large island
Grand Island
and joining again.
In the river, near
the Falls of Niagara
are many small islands:
Navy, Goat (formerly Iris) The Three Sisters, Little
Brother, Green, Bird, Juniper, Chapin, Crow, Rock,
Luna, Robinson, Cedar, Seldom Seen.

Goat Island splits the river into two
great falls: to the south, the Horseshoe,
north, the American. Luna sits here,
in a worn crease made by the folding,
on the brink of the American, the cascade
spilling down its south side
called The Bridal Veil.

There was a man who
was married on Luna,
who some thought
a trifle mad. It
wasn't that
(moonstruck)
not that at all

but a matter of attitude.

Knowing the moon to be out of his reach,
he submits to existence somewhere under it.
O yes love he is out there saying I do on Luna.

Below the falls the river
stretches north, to Ontario. It
is old, perhaps ten thousand years.

That it flows through a deep gorge below
the falls cannot be seen on the map,
or that there are rapids,
and bluejays in way down glens.

Along the river are cities, industries,
highways, homes, people. Over the river
there are bridges, and higher
yet, in night skies, the moon,
silvering everything.

They say that man will be on the moon
in three years. I do not believe them.

O

Man has been to the moon
and back. Three years have passed
during the writing of these lines.

I am here, you there, and I have seen
scrawled on the wall of a building

on Falls Street: *I am through trying*
to do something for this city

The building is slated for demolition.
It goes much the same for those among us
who plant flowers in holes in the roads,
paint the garbage cans pink.

O there is a great time coming, boys
with spanking new jeans for us all
money already in the pockets
and a rutabaga in every pot.
Yes, we have discount stores
shoeshine parlors, shopping malls
and a river of hydroelectric power.
It is an Electric City.

We also see the moon,
and have one way streets.

RECORD

Because you did not know the man
at least had not the vision I had
let this bear witness be record of
those eighty-some years

out of hills he came
not crawling, but upright
from PA and settled in Niagara Falls
with family in old farmhouse (on the out-
skirts, the rural side
of the railroad tracks

just why so moving those
hundreds of miles not
said, but it is known
that he delivered ice
driving two big bays
and worked for the city
putting in curbstones

finally being drawn back
to the wooded hills, the lumbering trade
following the camps from one part
of the country to the next

causing forests to crash down on themselves
stripping land bare, leaving stumps
(he worked at logging, operating the loader

and for the better part of those years
was not home at all.

Hellow Papa
I am waiting   Aug 22 1906
for you to come home   Burtsville Pa.

Oakes moved crost the railroad
good by.

Mamma is
filling the
lamp.

we are
looking
for you
home
why don't
you come

Hoping to see you soon
hant you got
the money
to come.
Mama made
a new dust
bag

Imim going to
get you somcandy

Well Otto we are
anxiously waiting
to get a line from   March 5 1908
you if you possibly   Mr. Otto McCoy
have the time   Dents Run
please let us hear   Penna.
from you soon
With love from all Ida

and later in that
year did come home
as seen by a postcard rec'd there

Dear Friend
The two engines
that were hailing
Me out of Buffalo   Oct 12 1908
were all smashed   Mr. Otto McCoy
to pieces in Buff   Tennessee Ave,
yards. Will you   Niagara Falls
save me a paper.   N.Y.
One man hurt
E.R.W.

it is also known
that there were three children
two girls, and one boy, the youngest

who later ran away to sea
escaping land forever
first Navy then Merchant Marine
these forty-odd years

and that both girls married
and the one that had a boy
and girl herself (in that order
died ten years after

and that he enjoyed a good hard drunk
of two or three days duration
even before all this

my father drove
on a summer Saturday
over the country roads
the two of them and me, nine
years old on the seat between them
stopping at the roadside bars
drinking and leaving for the next
how many miles away

stopping alongside the road
"When you get old," my father said
(us waiting in the car
him behind the wheel
"and you gotta go
you gotta go."

and of all the profound things
that fathers are supposed to say to sons
that (a farmhouse in the sunshine distance
wind in the bright green corn fields
birds warbling

was as good as any

and back in the car again
moving past woods and orchards
old barns leaning full of ache
to be part of the earth again
O we were going somewhere

and years later, did
down through Pennsylvania
two cars full of womenfolk,
and kids and one old man
stopping at a general store
way out in the back country
the only building out of six
(we were told
that stood there fifty years before
near a small village: Sinnamahoning.

(the kids on the porch
of the old store with soft drinks

"Your mother was born right over there."
(one of the women

pointing to sunlight in a clearing
and the remains of old foundations

and several old men sat on the steps
of the porch, and one in a rocker

(they too had followed
lumbering trails

"Ott," said the one in the rocker,
"do you remember the time you fell
off the top of the loader
and had to walk back to town?"

"Yes, dammit, I remember."

and so we got back in the cars
driving on, leaving the general store,
and those men a half century behind us.

out of all that happens
during a lifetime, there is little enough to speak of
and none left to tell again what is here taken note of
about a man who, in spite of, or in addition to, what
has been said here

(begot a family
of two girls one boy
chewed tobacco
came out of the hills

laughed when happy
cried when it was necessary
had a tumor the size of a fist
unfolding cut out of his back
lost the entire ring finger
of his right hand
worked, helped to pull down
the big forests
drank more than his share
and cursed mightily the whole time
the weather, work, and whiskey

was a gentle man
who died at eighty-two.

the lumber camps are for years silent
their harsh lines blurred with second growth

there remains but the hills to come out of
and the various ways out
this is one.

LOOKING FOR NIAGARA

It's Niagara lost
in the 20th century, disappeared
from the cereal box, up in mist,
a canvas backdrop in one hundred thousand
dead photographs, fading from postcards,
gone to Bermuda, Disney World, flown
to Aruba, splish took a bath at Niagara
splash went to Vegas for the weekend–
but had room at the motel
for Joseph and Marilyn
and were they impressed?
There's no record of it.

But the first human record at Niagara
before it had name–the first human at ?
who left a flint spear point, water
falling at the whirlpool then,
at old gorge, and the spear point:
dropped in fear, in awe,
in wonder at new water,
ice falling, who thought of it as !

Wandering hunter, archaeologists say, who
if he were there at all, didn't stay long,
as if he had, for months let's say, they'd
have known–would have found the tree
against which he relieved himself,
charcoal trace on stone, where he

cooked fish–as if no Niagara rock
has been left unturned.

The most recent evidence indicates he
did stay but a brief time–only minutes–
that dizzy from spoiled fish innards
he stumbled out of the woods
toward thunder, saw falling water, stared
slack-jawed into mists and steam rising
against south gorge wall, had visions:

The wall exploding, water rushing forth
gnawing south, divers fearful things–
dropped his spear, fled empty-handed
and throwing up back among the trees
and who wouldn't have?

What he saw: the sun rising and setting
3 million 647 thousand 445 times, ten
thousand winters and springs, trees
leafing out, hot suns, leaves coloring,
withering, dropping, snows whirling,
grass greening, fogs gathering, rains,
trees dying, toppling, new trees as slim
as spears growing thicker than his body,
salamanders mating between his gnarled toes,
mice nibbling algae from his ankles, a wolf
marking territory on his left shin

Caribou, mastodon, moose-elk, woods bison

wandering toward extinction. Mound Builders
heaping earth over the bones of their dead
a handful at a time until the mounds,
smoothed as round as breasts,
rose higher than their own heads,
were cloaked in green grass. The last Mound
Builders creeping past, without descendants
to put them safe to earth

The appearance of Attawandaronks, Algonkins,
Eries, Hurons, Senecas, Onondagas, Mississaugas,
Chippewas, Mohawks, Wyandots, Kahkwahs, Oneidas,
Wenroes, Tuscaroras, then streams of people
hide-covered, black-frocked, red-coated,
multi-clothed–the Seneca naming
the place Onguiaahra (Ne-uh-gar-uh):
throat, suffering Brule, the traitor playing
them, French and British against one another
until, tiring of his treachery, they
boiled and ate him and because
one is seldom enough tortured
Father Brebeuf to death (1648)
and ate him also, the earth spattering
into that dark and bloody ground surviving
battle-defeated Hurons, and tattooed
Neutrals whose tribe went beneath the earth,
rose into mist, Hinu, their thunder god
unable to save them

Father Hennipen proclaiming the Falls

to plunge 600 feet, "the great Fall"
swallowing "down all animals
which try to cross it, without
a single one being able to withstand
its current...[waters foaming and boiling
...thundering continuously]"

The Devil's Hole Massacre, where Senecas
cast wagon train and horses, clattering and rearing
over gorge edge, wagon wheels shattered roulette
sun-dial stopped, Merry-go-round, Ferris wheel,
eighty dead men sprawling with bloody skulls
scalps swinging in the shrieking air, those
who kept hair crumpled on rocks below–
survivors, two: Wagonmaster Stedman
who galloped toward the Falls to safety,
a drummer boy, tossed over the edge whose
drum straps caught in tree branches
who hangs there insensible, eyes
rolled back in his head

LaSalle's Griffin sucked toward Falls
on Maiden voyage, Iroquois chief Gironkouthie
taking LaSalle to Devil's Hole cave
where the voice of falling water
echoing in that stone mouth
foretold his death

Mrs. Simcoe belching and gorging herself
on sturgeon and whitefish, bragging

that the 5th Regiment had netted
one hundred sturgeon
and six hundred whitefish
in a single day
the seven hundred children of William Johnson
three by wife Mohawk Molly Brant
fanning out over the frontier
speaking in tongues, begetting
legions of tour guides who
aren't working the portage, the I-Am-Crawling-
On-All-Fours, no more, but who
walk backwards, working the tourists step
right this way, walk this way
to the famous waterfalls of Niagara–
and millions of tourists
are walking backwards

Fort Niagara and the House of Peace
being one and the same, 5000 Iroquois
clustered around the Fort winter of 1779
afterward known as Starvation Winter

General Brock in a coat as red
as a bullseye, sword waving, charging
up the hill to forever, Come on you
scoundrels, do you want to live–
taking a rifle-bullet heart-center
of the chest and spake
not another word, leaving
the question unfinished, to be asked

in another century
rising atop stone tower: Brock's Monument,
where he stands saluting those who later died
in Lundy's Lane, nearly three hundred up
on a funeral pyre of fence rails, the river
flowing, automobiles going beneath his stone gaze

An entertainment in which the schooner
Michigan, with "a cargo of ferocious wild
animals" was advertised to be floated over
the "falls of NIAGARA, 8th September, 1827,"
after the "greatest exertions...
to procure Animals of the most ferocious kind,
such as Panthers, Wild Cats and Wolves;
but in lieu of these, which it may be impossible
to obtain, a few vicious or worthless dogs,"
which turned out, on the day of the spectacle,
to be a bison, two bears,
two raccoons, one dog,
and a goose.
Twenty-five thousand people, who
knew what entertainment was when
they saw it, lined the riverbanks
cheering and gasping

the bison lowered its head, got
into defensive posture against the roar
of the thing with wide water-mouth, hooves
splintering deck planks as it
heaved to stay balanced

and then went down, swallowed
entire, far from the prairie,
though cheered by the crowd.

Bridges, following a kite string
suspending and cantilevering themselves
across the gorge, wooden beams clunking,
planks rattling, pine against oak, steel
girders clanging like wind chimes, cables
thrumming, everything hanging: trains,
troops, horses and carriages, trucks, cars.

Bridges appearing, changing names
to avoid detection, disappearing:
The Queenston & Lewiston
Suspension Bridge: Gone
The Lewiston Arch
The Niagara Suspension: Gone
The Railway Suspension: Gone
The Railway Arch, Grand Trunk Railway, Grand
Trunk Railway Arch, Lower Steel Arch, Lower
Arch, Whirlpool Rapids Bridge
The Railway Cantilever Bridge: Gone
The Michigan Central Railway,
The Canadian Pacific Railway
The Upper Steel Arch, The Falls View Bridge,
The Honeymoon Bridge: Gone
The Rainbow Bridge

Age taking some, wind taking some, and ice

taking the Honeymoon and the Honeymoon's
done–leaving the Rainbow
toward which we all run, arms spread,
ready to stumble over pots of gold,
over Canada, over Canaan, from where walked

The Reverend Josiah Henson, a head engineer
of the Underground Railway, over the 1850
Niagara Suspension, to meet Harriet
Beecher Stowe, who wrote the story he told:
Life Among the Lowly, though Henson's
name was Josiah, and he wan't no Uncle
Tom–he'd wangled seven hundred tickets
for fugitive slaves to ride
the Underground Line, sixteen
coaches long, pulling root cellars,
barns, secret rooms, shank's mare,
dark woods, owls hooting
campfires burning, fireplace logs and stove
wood snapping, torches flaring, candles
flickering, gas globe lamps glowing, canals
of Niagara growing–swung picks flashing,
shovelscrape, wheelbarrow roll, horses
leaning into harness creaking, got
a mule, gal, Sal, Erie Canal, low
bridge everybody down, the Hydraulic Canal
through the breast of town, accepting knives,
pistols and broken strong boxes, the flowing
of river water to generator, dynamo,
Barge Canal, Birth Canal, Love Canal

walk, canal talk, canal come out and play.

Lights in dance-hall gin-mill nights,
thousands of windows square and rectangle-
lighted, electric days, electric nights,
the air humming with currents, bulb-gleaming
network sky-dropped to the land,
street, search, spot, colored-lens
light on falling water and mist-mingle
smoke and vapor, the slam of steel on steel,
furnace roar, molten ore
puddling, eye-burning, face-searing,
pour splattering, foundry and coal,
titanium, chromium, all massing
in great memoriam, railroads chuffing,
wheel-squealing, freight moving, long
drawn whistle blowing, industrial hymn
of grimy shirts and pants working, who
hang on wash day lines, river water clean,
chlorine scented, blue sky, daring the breeze
to dance a little, take a little chance,
time of your life, time and a half.

River thick with daredevils
shooting the lower rapids in barrels,
boats, swimming, across the gorge
on tightropes, over the Falls–
understood, if it's big
whittle it down, stare at the shavings
wondering where it all went, domesticate

the wild, watch it caged until you
lose interest, if it's wisdom be
a clown until the oracle's language
is swallowed by laughter–or throw
yourself into its wide mouth, down
the throat–live or die, it can't
spit you out

then it's you, too, in history's glory
an eye-blink, mote, memory trace,
footnote, debris afloat eternally
in the cliché of time's river:

Sam Patch, jumper, in red trunks,
plunging down at attention, feet
first, arms at his sides, smiling
the 1829 prelim stunt to tightrope walkers:

Jean Francois Gravelet
aka The Great Blondin, aka The Prince
of Manila, the original thriller, the World's
Greatest Ropewalker, who walked the rope
in princely style, stood on one foot, perched
atop a chair, pushed a wheelbarrow, rode
a bicycle, walked at night, the tips
of his balancing pole marked by lights,
walked the rope with feet shackled in chains,
did somersaults, paused on the rope to take
pictures of the watching crowd, walked blind-
folded and, to the disappointment of gamblers,

who'd bet against him and cut supporting
wires mid-performance, carried his manager
across on his back, for which courage
Tuscaroras gave him gifts of beadwork.
Blondin's rival, Signor Guillermo Antonio Farini,
aka William T. Hunt, born in Lockport, N.Y.,
ropewalked also, stood on his head, walked
the line with a sack over his body,
lowered a bucket, pulled up water
for his Irish Washerwoman act,
while perched on rope in air.

Harry Leslie, aka The American Blondin,
Professor Jenkin, aka The Canadian Blondin,
across the rope on a velocipede.
Signor Henry Ballini, aka funambulist,
whose specialty was to lower himself
center-rope on a rubber strap,
an 1873 bungee, and jump into the river.

Steve Peer, whose unrepeatable trick
was to fall to his death.

Signorina Maria Spelterini, forward
and backward across the rope, with wrists
and ankles manacled, with peach baskets
on her feet, with a paper bag over her head.

Clifford Calverly, speedster, across the wire
in two minutes, thirty-two seconds, skipped rope

on the wire, hung by one foot, set off firecrackers.
Samuel J. Dixon, aka Daring Dixon, little flags
on the ends of his balancing pole, out on
the wire on one foot, lying down, hanging by
one hand–nearly the last of century's wirewalkers,
1890, earns $56.00 The approaching 20th century
turns away from balancing acts, yawns.

James Hardy, summer of 1896, several crossings,
The youngest of the tightrope walkers at 21 years
of age, and the last for 116 years.

Nik Wallenda, soft-shoeing in elk-skin slippers
over the wire, across the plunging Horseshoe Falls,
maw and gorge, through curtains of mist as heavy
as rain, shifting winds, from the U.S. to Canada,
one time, passport in waistband, 15 June 2012.

Barrel riders and others through the lower rapids
and Whirlpool: Carlisle Graham; George Hazlett
and William Potts, who rode together, then George
again, with his girlfriend Sadie Allen; Martha
Wagonfuhrer, Maud Willard and her dog (the dog
lived); the same day Willard died,
Carlisle Graham swimming the rapids;
Charles Percy in a boat;
Robert Flack in a boat,
died in the attempt;
Walter Campbell in a boat
with his dog, capsizes, dog drowns;

Peter M. Nissen, aka P.M. Bowser,
through the lower rapids
in the boat "Fool Killer."

William Kendall, aided
by a life jacket, swims the Whirlpool rapids;
Captain Matthew Webb, the first to swim
the English Channel, tries the Lower
Niagara, dies, red bathing trunks
flashing from the crest of the Forty Foot Wave;
James Scott, swimmer, dies.

And the Hill rapids riders:
Red Hill, Sr., Red Hill, Jr., and Major Hill,
tossing through the rapids in steel barrel,
through the rapids, evading the police
round the Whirlpool, and down
through the rapids in barrels again, down past
Niagara Glen, battered and bleeding, and taking
on water, and crawling out to drink a beer,
to smoke a big cigar.

A rapids run in rubber raft,
twenty-three dumped in, three drown;
Ken Lagergren kayaks through rapids
and four years later again with four
others; Robert Glenville and eight
others kayak the lower rapids.

Karel Soucek, twice through the lower

rapids in steel, wearing a red,
white and blue headband;
Dave Munday through the rapids, whirlpool,
and into the woods, eluding the police.

And the one who first went over the Falls:
Annie Edson Taylor, in a wooden barrel
in which she'd sent a kitten, as a test,
ignoring its death because, even by her
reckoning, she was no kitten.

Bobby Leach, who took the trip in steel, took
a beating, breaking bones, his kneecaps, his jaw,
who sat on his barrel for a photograph, wearing
a bow tie and elastic bands around his white
shirt sleeves to keep his cuffs at the proper length,
who sat by the riveted hatch, holding a knobby cane.

Charles Stephens, who strapped himself
in a wooden barrel, feet to the ballast anvil,
who on impact shot through barrel-bottom
and died, leaving an arm tattooed
Forget Me Not, still strapped inside,
as if to wave goodbye to the waiting crowd.

Jean Lussier, in a rubber ball, 4th of July
1928, came out smiling, waving flags,
the Union Jack, the Stars and Stripes

George L. Stathakis, who wrote *The Mysterious*

Veil of Humanity through the Ages, who took
a pet turtle named Sonny Boy with him
over the brink, who spent nearly a day
behind the falling water–suffocated.
The turtle lived, but told no tale.

Red Hill, Jr., carrying silver dollars
a piece of the Blarney Stone, and a four-
leaf clover, went over in a barrel of inner
tubes, webbing, and net, but had no luck,
barrel going to pieces on impact–Hill
floating to the surface a day later.

William A. Fitzgerald, aka Nathan T. Boya, who
said he did it for "very, very personal reasons,"
over in a rubber ball: the Plunge-O-Sphere,
patterned after Lussier's ride.

Karel Soucek, in 1984, in a red barrel,
"Last of Niagara's Daredevils" painted on it,
who said afterward, "I feel fine."

Steven Trotter, in August 1985, in modified
end-to-end pickle barrels patterned after Hill's.
Trotter sits relaxed on Gazette front page:
in checkered trunks, one leg crossed at the knee,
sun glasses around his neck, he's smiling, displaying
newspaper headlines of his plunge in one hand, the
other making a thumb's up sign
as if he's hitchhiking a ride

somewhere, or reviewing the movie of his life.
The youngest, at 22, to ever perform this feat.

John D. Munday, in Oct 1985, carrying a rabbit's foot
and a silver dollar, whose barrel on which was painted
"To Challenge Niagara," was hoisted into the water
above the Falls with the help of six tourists,
who had no idea he was inside.

Peter DeBemardi and Jeffery Petkovitch,
Sept 1989, over the Horseshoe Falls
in the same barrel, equipped with oxygen tanks,
strap-hammocks, Plexiglas windows, and a video
camera. "Don't Put Yourself on the Edge–Drugs Will
Kill" it says on the barrel. "Like a roller coaster
ride...straight down," Petkovitch says afterward.
They stand together in the Gazette photo:
DeBernardi with unbuttoned shirt and mustache,
Petkovitch with an arm around his shoulder,
smiling, a cowboy hat on his head.

Jessie W. Sharp, June, 1990, over
the Horseshoe to his death in red kayak,
"Rapidman" stenciled on it in black.

The return of Steven Trotter, accompanied
this time by Lori Martin, on Father's Day, 1995,
over the Horseshoe, the first man and woman
to ride over together.

Robert Overacker, October 1995, having attending
stunting school, attempts to survive a jet-ski ride
over the Horseshoe, parachuting to safety as he
clears the brink–but chute fails. He dies.

Oscar Williams, 1910, starts over a cable strung
across the gorge near the Upper Suspension Bridge
when–suddenly–it sags, and halfway across
he's trapped in the center of the drooping cable,
clinging on for dear life, as they say, hanging
there for a half hour until he's rescued
by being lowered to the Maid of the Mist
boat waiting below.

Kirk Raymond Jones, October 2003: goes over the
Horseshoe Falls with nothing but the clothes he wears,
No barrel, no life-preserver, no nothing, the ultimate
dare to the devil–and lives, unharmed. A tourist
interviewed onsite that day said, "I don't think he set
a very good example, especially for kids."

Me going, looking for Niagara, believing
what's lost might still be sound, checking
out the Lost and Found, sending invitations–
let us go then me and you or was it you
and I? while smokestacks and observation
towers stick up into the haze
of the helicoptered sky like spears
in the soft gut of a slow dumb
dying beast shambling invisible

through tourist crowd, always
in the background the falling water
sound, a shroud down over rock face,
mist rising straight up, a signal seen
for miles and miles, here, right here,
this is the place, though Twain saw it
as paradise lost, and poked fun at it,
though Hawthorne had to go at it
more than once before he got it,
though Whitman didn't even try,
but described it from inside
a train, sitting on a bridge,
and Dickens broke off a piece of its rock
thinking he could take it home with him.

Well, Charlie, I want that rock back.
Some descendant or other of yours has it,
at the bottom of some trunk, or high
on a shelf, or sinking forgotten
into the ground of an English garden–
so you and yours stand accused
and there'll be no pardon until it's back
here, cemented on from where it split off
at the smack of that hammer. Where do
you get off, anyway? Just because you can
write a little doesn't mean you can bust
up pieces of the New World, of Niagara,
and carry them away.

Me going along the escarpment, over rock,

between trees, gorge at my back, shoes torn,
left sole flapping, tied with string,
looking for some sign, for a footprint,
for anything–there's a hawk drifting,
riding the current down over the Million
Dollar Highway, the vineyards, looking, too,
and it's dark when I pull up over the top
go cross-country onto Tuscarora land,
heading toward music, stumble
into festival as if into dream, fires
burning, moon floating above the horizon
and Allen Ginsberg's there talking
to a girl who wants to write, who's
asking How do I get the moon
into a poem? while it's shining pale
light into her face and Ginsberg's
saying gently, Write the moon.

That's it, for sure, but while he's standing
smiling beatifically there's this moon soaring,
this hunter's, harvest, beyond supergibbous
halved-muskmelon moon, this full and gorgeous
heart-break, honey dripping honeymoon
Niagara moon hanging in the black sky
as pretty as anything ever done on velvet.
It's a vampire moon, a werewolf moon,
enough to make anybody, or anything, throw
back its head, or whatever it's got, and howl.

And it's me going again, dogs whooping it up

way back in the dark, foxes barking, coyotes
crying, owls hooting, all manner of howling
at my back, even the wolf-spiders and sunflowers
and goldenrod raising their reedy voices,
and the snakes, and eels, the turtles, the toads
and frogs, a hoarse and treble screaming and snipe
keening in night thickets, ghost bear roaring,
deer snorting and blatting, the fish poking
stiff jaws and pouting mouths out of the water
and sputtering a cold chorus, lovers
and those who aren't lovers tossing
their heads back and making noises, babies
wailing, and the dead whispering–a great
clashing, caterwauling, yowling howl for Niagara.

From reservoir's top, waiting river water
awash with the rippling sound, with moonlight,
high tension towers stalking spread-legged
and stiff-armed holding up their lines, me going
past under them, scrambling flap-soled over roads,
railroad tracks, through fields, shoe-mouth
jamming full of torn grasses, and breathless
me accepting a bag of smelt from fishermen
walking with lanterns and flashlights
near the river now, it's been a bloody run,
the Falls falling, with that nighttime,
car-horn, wind-chime in the ear calling,
sneaking, wild howling in the memory,
shoe aflop down the streets where
the tourist-dressed are strolling, who

look up at buildings, around in space,
at the moon, with puzzlement of face
Where, they're asking the air, is it?

And do I point toward rumble, say
Over there? Who'd care? I'm waiting
for my vision, too, cooking for it,
got a trash fire going in a pothole
near the curb where old Whirlpool turns
toward the Falls, got smelt frying
in a garbage can lid, taking a sit
on the curbstone, poking fire with a stick,
looking for a hit of dioxin, PCBs, lead,
mirex, nickel, acid, grass, crack, crank,
smack, tossing back my fourth smelt
with beer, when the cops pull up.

The flash of tourist cameras
attracted them: I got a sign on cardboard
says "Niagara's Underclass," grease running
down my chin, burrs in my hair, mud smeared
pants, a howl in the back of my throat,
a shoe that looks ready to talk. I'm
feeling, in other words, right at home.

Released on my own running recognizance, I'm
pounding through back lots, yards, hitting berms
and medians before I realize they're back there
laughing, not in pursuit–they've got what's left
of my smelt, and they have other flakes to fry.

Me circling back, going toward the Falls finding
deserted streets, alleys, watching for headlights
behind, for piles of garbage, discarded mattresses
ahead, where I'd throw myself if a car hit the alley,
where I'd be just somebody sleeping one off,
or just another body waiting for collection,
another casualty of urban renewal.

Over the night barricades and across
the old bridge to Goat Island, sticking to the trees,
an imagined woods in the dark, sneaking in and out
of a moon-soaked clearing where Red Jacket sits
patiently, dew on his hair, small round likeness
of George Washington around his neck, waiting
for dawn, for the artist to reappear,
to finish painting his picture–
his eyes following me across the clearing,
me going across the road into the brush
toward the brink of the Falls, looking
down, not to see it until the last.

Shuffling slow through a half century
of disintegrating flash bulbs crunching
under my feet, my broken sole, bulbs and cubes,
ankle-deep in a litter of film wrappers and foil–
lifting my eyes to the slick beast leaping thick
with wonderment, swans and snakes, beauty
of plumage and scale curving over the edge
in mindless thundering, terrible fear

of graceful necks and flow of body relentlessly
plunging, growling, throaty, swallowing all,
everything down in the unseen dark right beside
me, for a moment only–then gone to water
flowing behind an aluminum railing.

Lifting my disposable lighter
in the dark, and flicking, thumbsore,
for no flame, not even a single birthday
candle flicker. Nothing sustains, nothing
found forever and I'm dropping my wheel and flint
into the litter around my feet, into the linger
of original wonder, and turning stumbling back
to the streets and houses of the world.

A GOOD WAR

The golden afternoon wars
against night, slow motion

bumblebees crisscross
the back yard, droning like gilded

bullets, plunging into
the red hearts of hollyhocks
along the fence.

And along the old railroad
station, troop trains rumble
in, school children

are waving flags and the young
soldiers are looking out from behind
the streaked windows, and people

lining the track
are cheering and weeping–
and everyone goes home
to flatten out tin cans
and to grow Victory gardens.

*

Across the continent,
which stretches out before us

like a lesson in geography,
and also the sea, of course,
there is a war going on

bombs rupture
the land into dark
blossoms of earth, each
with its red center, mortars
tear the veined afternoon
into ragged pieces–cities turn
into a blaze of flower gardens

and here, in the quiet summer,
butterflies, and occasionally
a Piper Cub pulled by

its fluttering propeller, floats
through its leisurely blue–once
in a while a fluffy white cloud.

*

In the backyard gardens
tracer-bullet dragonflies
glint in the lemon sunlight
zip in oblique angles
over staked tomato plants.

A lowered arch of sunrays
bombards the backyards, shadows

dig in behind the shrubberies.

The activities of armies cease,
except scouts on patrol, who
move cautiously in the dark gardens

whining for blood, and the shell-
shocked moths, blundering
in the yard, batting themselves
into frayed unconsciousness
against the window screen.

                    *

And over those amber fields of grain
those caissons
keep rolling
along

and Johnny
is marching home again
Hurrah! Hurrah! Johnny
keeps marching home
again, while over
there, over

there, our boys
are going through
bombs bursting in air
giving proof through the night

up on 56th Street is a dim saloon
with faded and paint-peeling sign
and the name of the saloon is

The Seabees where
from 1942 to 46 the smoke hung
under the bright lights beer, whiskey
and hard laughter.

       *

And now I in my father's house
sprawled out in bed, the weeds
in the backyard garden
long years brown
and dead, think

of putting a patio in, with
redwood deck, barbecue grill,
badminton net. What

good times we
will have. How the laughter
will jump high into the blue
over the net, the birdie
drifting back and
forth.

Three jets, one after the other
thunder the night apart, the noise

hanging in the distance a long while
before the horizon muffles it.

The front lines keep changing
and it is difficult to keep up.

A good war, I am thinking
is a hard thing to find

LOCUST SONG & WINE

Suddenly
it is summer
and we, in our late
twenties, are old.

Four or five of us out
of the old neighborhood
sit in the shade on my
front porch and drink
Paisano from jelly glasses.

Out on the sidewalk
under the hot sun
the proud young girls walk by
flashing sleek indolent calves.

We talk about women–
"You know," Hugh Murphy
says, tilting the gallon
and splashing red wine
into his glass, "Catholic
girls are the best lovers.

They have that dark sorrow,
and such a profound sense
of original sin."

Later, after more wine
we talk about baseball.

Part Two: What I Want

COUNTRY

It was not love
at first, among tender
rows of new corn. Or even
last, it was not, watching
burnished apples drop
into the hard frost.
Yet more than sexual
attraction held
at arm's length
for a summer.

It persisted until fall,
until the loft grew deep
with sweet hay, with dusk–
the young farm girl armed
with trust, following
down evening lanes,
small even milk teeth
smiling, wanting
to know what
love is.

And I, eager
to be away, ahead
of winter crashing
downward like an age,
gave no answer. And having
given none, packed what was

mine into the car, and drove off.

It was unsaid, undone,
what came away with me. It was
like a swath of wheat left uncut
at one end of the field suddenly
remembered after the first snow.
The country remains as it was,
suspended, a land of summer
between cities

OPEN BOOK

At the onset it was between the lines,
then held, secret, secure, under layers
of meaning, in words. The book of the bed
gapes open, from its white page we rise,
the meat of the text, indecipherable words
struggling to articulate ourselves.
Read me. Read me.

And finally, words can not contain us,
we play in the margin of the page,
ready to leap into eternity,
into that infinite space
that is not even white.
We rise into the universe,
into each other, filling
crack and crevice
of the room.

Who among us
can say what love is, that we
are not gods, are not eternal?
An ambulance that wails outside,
rising and falling, pulls us down
to the street. The wind blows chill.

The world is, after all,
real. I make, with my body
a parenthesis, enclosing sleep.

DRAGONFLY

And so we moved
to an old place in the country
hauling, between the two of us, boxes
and boxes of books, none of which

I have looked at again. For three
years I have been watching the countryside,
staring at its massed summer green, seeing
the bones of the land push through in autumn.
Reluctantly, the old farm reveals itself:

In the woods, an overgrown orchard,
betrayed by its blossom, comes visible
the pear trees, hung with wild grapes,
continue to bear a crop which is dropped
to the ground, harvested by raccoons
and birds. On the edge

of the woods quince trees struggle
through the aspen to offer their bitter
misshapen fruits to the sun,
and along the creek bottom

runs an old strand
of barb-wire, rusty claws fixed
firmly in the past, held fast by maples
whose trunks have grown around it.

The wire and trees insist
that old boundaries remain, that things
be kept as they were–the creak of leather
harness, the snort and stamp of the horse
pulling the plow, the small man walking
behind, up over the hill, narrow
brown furrow following in
the green, the dinner
bell ringing.

The horse, though, laid down
in the pasture one sunny morning
fifty-odd years ago
and died. The man,

too, some years later,
the one who strung the wire,
shrunken smaller still, tired
of farming, of walking
and walking over again
that same land, died
quietly in bed

while his son rode up
and down the south forty
on a tractor.

The old plowshare was never
beaten into a sword, or anything
else. Chipped a little, on its leading

edge, it rests quietly among the pear trees
in the woods.

The harness, or pieces
of it, rot into the ground
near what was once the milkhouse,
buckles and iron rings crusted thick
and inarticulate with rust. Grass
covers them.

The barb-wire–the taut strand running
swift through the woods like a melancholy
harp string–keeps nothing in
or out:

Woodchucks scurry under it without
looking up, the occasional hunter glances
once and walks the line to where
it is gone.

A fox passes by
in the winter–his prints
meander to their own
pattern, paying no heed
to the wire.

The wind
as it rushes through
plays a cruel tune on it,
and even the black raspberry

has, in half a century, come down
the hill, and wandered out.

I do not violate
the boundary, but keep
to the green woods where even the air
seems green, sunlight pulsing
through the leaves.

A faded cow path
trails off among the trees,
loses itself.

A short distant
away, in the hollow,
the bones of the cow rest,
half embedded in the earth, mossy,
scattered by the wilderness, unread

waiting to be read,
waiting for the seer
to see them there, before
ivy erases their portent
for another summer.

High overhead a jet draws
a streak of sunlit white, its point
a tiny glitter of tinfoil in the sky.
It races toward the future
ahead of its own sound.

I try to decide if
it too is beautiful.

For an instant the insects stop
humming, suspended in sunlight–
a dragonfly hangs in the air
on an invisible thread,
bi-winged, lost, out of time,
an early prototype
of things to come.

I decide that it is.

On the edge of the woods
the yellow globes of the quince
leap out of the green, pale
replicas of the sun.

FARMHOUSE PORCH

From the farmhouse
porch the sunlight
is over the pasture
like distilled amber

insect humm

across the fields
some one chops wood.

SPARROW

take the image of
a frantic sparrow sealed
in a thermos bottle

how long after
the air gives out can
the most delicate instrument
detect warmth inside?

what the temperature of so
small a breath exhaled in
a chamber dark and oblong,
fragile glass, designed
to hold hot coffee
or tea?

let us not
be conventional
let us drink sparrows
with our noon meal, wash
down our liverwurst sandwiches
with the warm song of sparrows,
and go back to work at one o'clock,
gasping for air.

WHAT I WANT

I want you to pay attention
I want to be a good American
I want to know who I have to kill
and how many
I want the best money can buy
I want to know how much it costs
I want to know if I can get it wholesale
I want to know how much down
I want to put it on layaway
I want my money back
I want somebody to tell me yes,
money does grow on trees
I want people who say, "You think I'm made
out of money?" to discover that they are
I want their faces to turn green,
surprised George Washingtons
I want In God We Trust
to be across the backs of their heads
I want rolled coins to be some part of their anatomies
I want burglars to sneak into their bedrooms
and tear off parts of their bodies while they sleep
I want to work a double
I want to hear America singing
I want to hear Joe Cocker sing Amazing Grace
I want to go the heaven without dying
I want to go just for a visit,
for a long weekend to see if I like it
I want someone to promise

that smoking will never hurt me
I want someone other than *Phillip Morris Magazine*
to promise that smoking will never hurt me
I want my doctor to say, "Oh, up to a pack
and a half a day never hurt anybody."
I want eating pickled possum feet more than twice
a week to be the only thing that causes cancer
I want this to be discovered by reading the message
left by the possum's star-shaped footprints
I want saloons that sell pickled possum feet to be
required to post a warning on the sides of the jars
I want everybody to love everybody else
and have long, happy, and rewarding lives–
except for people I don't like
I want them all to drop dead
as soon as I finish this list
I want to practice these I Wants until they start
to sound like Ray Charles singing What I Say
I want backup singers I want to call them
the What I Want Singers,
What I Want
I want them to have stars in their eyes
I want them to wear tight red, white, and blue dresses
I want a pen pal from another galaxy
I want Detroit to give me that secret carburetor
that gets 1000 MPG
I want to be granted just one wish
I want a wishing ring that works
I want you to know that the idea
of the hula hoop was stolen from me

I want recognition also for the pencil
sharpener, the paper clip, and the zipper
I want that woman in the red dress
I want trees to scream and spurt blood
when they're cut
I want to buy the next round
I want to buy Mother Cabrini another martini
I want a long-legged woman to bring me another beer
I want you to know there are people
in this world who don't like you
I want you to know someone
is watching your house
I want to know the whereabouts of Jimmy Hoffa
I want wages to be replaced entirely
by graft, bribes, payoffs, kickbacks
I want all animals to talk
I want them to tell fabulous stories
about when the earth was young
I want to have a meaningful
relationship with a mink
I want to exterminate phrases like meaningful
relationship, interface, input, output, feedback,
hands-on, empowered, co-dependent, and so on
I want people to see beauty and intelligence
in every other animal they previously
thought ugly and stupid
I want people to see the beauty in one another
I want them to have special glasses
to help them do this
I want these glasses to be called eyes

I want your vote
I want all the Richards of the world
to have the courage to be known as Dicks:
Dick Nixon, Dick Burton, Dick Gere, Dick
the Lion Hearted, Dick Little, Little Dick, and so on
I want a two-way wrist radio
I want something magical to happen when I say,
Shazam!
I want Submarine Man to surface
and become a member of Greenpeace
I want to have a lotta nerve
I want to have a lotta gall
I want to have a lotta balls
I want some scratch
I want it known that Americans have 312 terms
that refer to money and that snow might be one of them
I want that woman in the white dress
I want to wear my Good Conduct Ribbon
wherever I go
I want my friends to grow up
I want my friends to wake up
I want my friends to stand up and be counted
I want my friends to sit down and shut up
I want to be consistent
I want to contain multitudes
I want to come out of the cradle endlessly rocking
I want infants to be receptive to toilet training
at three weeks
I want them to signal their parents by holding up
one or two fingers at the proper time

I want to paint the ceiling of the Astrodome
with pictures of starving children
I want athletes to have their annual salaries
and a list of their sports injuries
printed on their uniforms
I want candy bars to cost 5 cents
I want spurs that jingle-jangle-jingle
I want to remember the Red River Valley
I want to be back in the saddle again,
back where a friend is a friend
I want to feel at home on the plains
where the deer and the antelope play
I want to hear that discouraging word
I want people to stop trying to sell me
replacement windows and above-ground pools
I want people with eternity in one hand to stop
smiling and knocking on my door
I want that woman in the blue dress
I want to take a tour of the St. James Infirmary
I want there to be a sin-tax on blacktop and concrete
I want to fight the good fight
I want to donate my Purple Heart to the VFW
I want my old injuries to stop hurting in bad weather
I want my old injuries to stop hurting in good weather
I want a woman to help me off with my boots,
one for each foot
I want them to go to college to learn
how to do it right
I want them to go to trade school
if they flunk out of college

I want Stephen W. Hawking to admit
he got all his ideas from me
I want there to be capital punishment for killing time
I want science to find all the answers
I want technology to save my soul
I want painless dentistry to be a fact
I want it discovered that Liberace
wrote all those Muddy Waters' tunes
I want to get my mojo working
I want yo mama
I want to do it for Old Glory
I want a woman with three breasts
to be my personal secretary
I want this to be required reading in high schools
I want to remember 700 funny jokes
that nobody heard before
I want them all to start with the line,
"Man walks into a haberdashery."
I want my friends to stop hitting on my wife
I want my friends to stop hitting on my girlfriend
I want them to realize when I
hit on their wives and girlfriends
that it's different.
I want them to mind their own business
I want people to stay out of my way
I want people to stop talking about me
I want people to stop laughing behind my back
I want them to hear my 700 jokes: man walks
into a haberdashery...Take my life–please
I want R.E.S.P.E.C.T.

I want egg in my beer
I want to know who stole the kishke
from the butcher shop
I want Charles Bukowski to be resurrected
and to spend another lifetime teaching Sunday School
I want to be good with my hands, real good
I want to be able to weld Kryptonite
to frankincense using an incense stick
I want the leak in my garage roof to fix itself
I want geneticists to discover irrefutable proof
that every person on earth has ancestors who were:
African, Arab, Argentinean, Armenian, Balinese,
Brazilian, British, Czechoslovakian, Danish, French,
German, Greek, Hispanic, Hungarian, Indian, Irish,
Israeli, Italian, Japanese, Korean, Lebanese, Mexican,
Moroccan, Maltese, Native American, Norwegian,
Outer Mongolian, Palestinian, Polish, Qatarian,
Rumanian, Scottish, Spanish, Swedish, Turkish, Texan,
Ukrainian, Visigoth, Varangian, Vogel, Welsh,
Xanthenes, Xenophobic, Yugoslav, and Zulu
I want that woman in the pink dress
I want UFOs to be registered with the DMV
I want ex-addicts to stop telling their stories on TV
I want the word "crepuscular" to refer
to a certain lack of muscle tone
I want what it takes
I want a couple of minutes
to get my thoughts together
I want to get organized
I want to know who really killed JFK

I want Electroman to touch my shoulder
with his magic wand, proclaiming,
"LIIII-VE FOREVER!"
I want Stephen King to start writing nonfiction
where the greater horror is found daily
I want everybody to know that no news is no news
I want a bird in the bush to be worth two in the hand
I want every President to be given sodium pentathol
once a year during a special hour-long *Nightline*
I want a telepoll immediately afterward
to determine if anyone could tell the difference
I want to get Georgia off my mind for as little while
I want to ride the Wabash Cannonball
drinking coffee and smoking big cigars
I want to invent a perfume that smells
like bed-sheets fresh off the clothesline
I want the wind always at my back
I want that Michael Jackson key chain
the one with Van Gogh's ear on it
to be sold on ebay
I want satellite photography to reveal a great text
written by whales on the bottom of the Atlantic
I want it to be obvious that the Dead Sea Scrolls
were plagiarized from this text
I want the bones of a whale
and the skeleton of a man with one leg
to be uncovered together at a NJ construction site
I want to be an automotive gardener
I want to plant the voltage regulator from a 1951 Ford
in my backyard and grow a brand new 1951 Ford

I want you to know my needs are modest
I want to recommend somebody for Sainthood
I want to start taking applications
as soon as I finish this list
and all the people I don't like drop dead
I want to keep on saying what I want until the end
of the century, the end of the world, or for another
half hour–whichever comes first
I want it all
I want to give it all away
I want to take a break
I want to make a complaint
I want that woman to stop looking at her watch
I want to know what color dress
she thinks she's wearing
I want you to know that we consider ourselves winners
even though we lost the election
I want to thank you all for your support. Thank you.
Thank you. Thank you.

Part Three: Finding Niagara

NIAGARA REVISITED

And still there
are more things left unsaid
than have been said. The city
is a poem that keeps revising itself

–I turned down a ticket to see Elvis who
in scuffed blue suede, heels run down,
will soft shoe at the new
Convention Center

in Niagara Falls. Slowly
I turn step
by step
retrace my steps

Third street gone, The Silver
Dollar gone, the Rayot gone,
gone the people who
holy with incandescent light
marched with torches in the streets
in celebration of electricity
gone construction workers who
marched with beer from bar
to bar building Robert Moses
Hydroelectric gone

–now marching step
by step, under bright lights

taken for granted, the young women in
the U.S.A. Beauty Pageant, their smiles
so large that they roll them,
like old-fashioned hoops
onto the stage

and not one of them
in response to the question, says
"I think the greatest person in the world
was Daring Dixon! Cliff Calverley! Nicola Tesla!"
(they also gone

and I too am going and as I go
look over my shoulder down Main, where
far off, almost lost in a dazzle of streetlight
a white-haired man dismounts from a white horse,
tying its reins to a parking meter,
I am going, going
gone, for a dollar plus change
like a box of assorted nuts
and bolts at a country auction,
like the poem my friend wrote
nearly forty years ago:
"Over Niagara On A Bird."

Only the title remains.
The poem gone, what
the bird flew over

gone. A word like

a heavy bell, he's
not dead
he's gone.
Gone home. Gone
beyond. Gone
to his great reward.

The sound of breathing gone
the Amazing Dr. Zarcon's Breathing Machine
fallen to pieces and resurrected
one more time.

Out of all the waiting
and watching, no tracks in the snow,
no breathing, no lair.
Fragments. Everything
gone.

And yet I'm telling myself
it's got to be a new city
I'm telling myself.
I'm telling myself.
I'm telling myself.

NICOLA TESLA DREAMING ON GOAT ISLAND

In Yugoslavia at the age of six he dreamed
about Niagara and a waterwheel–and years
later dreamed of throwing electricity all
over the world, without wires, to far planets,
people taking what they needed from the air–
Tesla, who championed the alternating current
that lights the earth, who drove Edison mad,
who drove Edison into the public electrocution
of cats and dogs at lectures to demonstrate
the satanic danger of alternating current–
Tesla, who invented the radio before Marconi,
who held computer patents in the 1800s, who
believed high voltage cables running under
classroom floors would stimulate the intellect
of dull students. Who, during the last years
of his life, became a caretaker of park pigeons,
feeding them, even from between his lips,
as they fluttered around his feet, alighted
on his hat, his shoulders, his outstretched
arms, a Saint Nicola of Alternating Current,
gone to the birds. Who now sits brooding
in bronze on Goat Island, larger than life,
still attracting the occasional pigeon as he
sits, open book on his lap, pretending to read
but looking over the heads of wandering tourists
to watch the rush of water surging toward the Falls,
the volume diminishing over the years–dreaming
that soon all the water will stop flowing,

that it will all be turned into electricity,
transforming the earth into a planetary fireball
of lightning, illuminating the furthest reaches
of the dark universe, beyond our imaginations.

WILD GEESE FLY UPRIVER

Notes toward narrative

That a river could
do it, not to talk daredevils
but a man who quit (was fired
from several jobs

for not showing up, or when
he did, for spending mornings
in the shop, sparks flying
from the grinding wheel, making
steel barbs for spear fishing

for leaving at lunchtime
returning at quitting time
handing out fish to the men
coming out through the gate

a man who finally gave up all pretense
and went to live beside it a year

(the lower Niagara, subdued
but still roaring through
its gorge in this century

and before that, huge water up
in one place: The Forty Foot Wave

(where Captain Matthew Webb disappeared
in July 1883, trying to swim the rapids

(three days later
drifting into shore at Lewiston
some five miles downstream.

It could do that easily enough
and keep murmuring that it wasn't at fault
could come bearing unexpected gifts
bring news of an old lover
still faithful, in memory
after all these years

and the gift given the man who
looked long at the river
into the swiftwater.

He was divorced (his wife
having gone off in the same direction
as his jobs, or rather

both wife and jobs remaining
stationary and he going off
in his own direction

but at any rate
divorced.

and so in the river gorge

remade his story that summer
hunting up old railroad timbers
and driftwood, building
himself a shelter (you
had to get down on hands
and knees to crawl in–
packing cases of beer
over miles of rocky trail
building stone by stone
out into the river
a spearing dock.

The water crashes after itself, filling
the gorge with a noise that cancels
speaking. You shout to be heard

but "what we have piled up here"
is water and there's nothing mysterious
in that–water is water

varying only in intensity.
Niagara comes out of your faucet, he
said. To look out over Lake Ontario
when the wind is pulling the big waves up
is to look out over any ocean, he said.

(he had never seen an ocean
but no matter.

He lived at gorge bottom

through that winter (spearing

three or four hours a day
reddened hands gripping the pole,
staring into swift water

where beneath the surface
Captain Webb kept going by
as pale as ice, head first
feet first, one arm flung
out, still swimming
against the current

and the rest of the time
huddled up in lean-to
prodding the smoky fire
frying up the stray fish
his spear tines found
(sleeping

The snow lay deep in the gorge
that year, for days he saw no one
(long nights clear and cold overhead
the bitter blink of stars.

And times then B. Levering and I
hunting rabbits, eased over
the lip of the gorge
into that depthless white
called more by descent

than hope of game

and find (by smoke
the warm center
of all that unmarked snow.

Crowded into
that small space
we'd drink coffee,
hold fingers to the fire

Rabbits? he'd say
Last week was it? I had three
or four hanging in that tree out there

and back outside

You shoulda been here yesterday!

(now he is relieving himself
in the general direction
of the river, free
arm waving wild
descriptions
in the air:

Was a blizzard and wild geese
came flying upriver over the rapids–
musta been thirty–whadda thing to see!

the snow coming down!

The last four trips below we
hear the story of the geese again
and again
just yesterday
just yesterday
shoulda been
here a day earlier

and then winter was over.

The man climbed up out of the gorge
went to live with his married sister
in a place they fixed for him, up
under the third floor roof–
there was a cot and quilts, it
was cozy there his sister said.

In the spring, kids exploring
the gorge trashed the lean-to, flung
the frying pan into the rapids, crushed
the coffeepot, trampled the ripped blankets
into the mud, and set fire to what was left.

Up in a third floor cubbyhole he
dozes on the evening cot, dreaming
he's in the lower river, water
above his knees, rope around
his waist to a tree on shore–miles

downriver a sturgeon turns upstream
toward the hinged points of his spear,
Captain Webb rides the crest
of the Forty Foot Wave, wild
geese are flying overhead.

Heavy spring rain gurgles
and crashes after itself
in the downspout, restless
pigeons coo up under the eaves,
ruffling their wings in the damp.

FINDING NIAGARA

It's tough to tell, isn't it, where Niagara hid
when you were a kid, and didn't come out till now?
Could have been in the Cave of the Winds, the largest
wind instrument on the Frontier, could have been
in the Winter Garden, now put to rest, where I once
stood in front of a greenhouse audience and read
poetry amid the rock and water pools, but
I don't think so.

It got small, is what, and messed up and slept
in the backseat of an abandoned car for a time,
then under a viaduct out of the sleeting rain,
then years in a closed-up building, windows
plywooded over, as empty and as forgotten
as a discarded postcard from 1956
in the gathering dust there on the floor,
where a slant of summer sunlight finds
it once a day for eight minutes or a little
more, on a day when sunny fortune shines.

It fades in summer heat, is as cold
as any other bloodless thing in winter.
It hears a loud voice saying, "I don't pay
you what I owe on Friday, I'll kiss your ass
on Main Street, right here, Niagara Falls, NY!"
and the reply, "Big deal. Who'd see?"
If it could have laughed, it would have.
But it was too tired.

***

It fell to pieces, it did, and hid
all over the place. It hid on the railroad
tracks, it joined the Army, crept into potholes,
sparkled along the edges of broken glass, went
to community college and took truck-driving classes,
collected unemployment, swore it was looking
for work, smoked a little dope, drank a few beers,
saw itself expanding into the universe
in shimmering particles, knew it was busted
up bad, tossed into garbage cans, trucked and dumped
into a landfill, where flocks of seagulls soared
and whirled above, sunlight glinting from their wings,
crying out to one another–
they knew Niagara when they spied it.

***

Clouds swirling over Niagara, mare's tails, kites flying
against blue skies, nothing but blue skies, empty,
darks clouds moving in from the west people say,
distant musket fire, rain unceasing, and pieces
creeping out of hiding, inching toward the Falls.
This is a journey that takes years.

The pieces go night and day, misshapen snails
that leave veins of silver trailing across the pavement,
some are crushed by cars, some burn in the fire of urban

renewal, but they continue,
one generation after the next,
they are coming together
as if they are stories being passed on,
all heading toward the river above the Falls.
Like wilted flowers, chunks of stars, dust of old
factories, fox teeth, petrified tears, they are
swept over the brinks of the Horseshoe,
the American, the Bridal Veil, where
a music pounds to fuse them forever.

***

It's got to be Dr. Sax, know what I'm saying?
the one from Belgium, yes, but also the book
by the guy born in Lowell, that book with The Great
Snake in it, one of the many stories about snakes,
snakes in the garden, snakes in the grass, snakes
get a bad rap, still Lawrence made one flee, but felt
regrets, and Emily had her "narrow fellow," snakes
intertwined with worship and evil for tens of thousands
of years–and we hear that Niagara story, the Indian
woman plunging in grief, a variation, saved and
lowered gently, a fire and smoke and a snake, a story
that shifts and flows beyond printed word, that won't
be trapped, a spoken story that once spoken, rises
in mist and hides and settles to be told again, renewed.

It is a story concealed behind cascading water,
one most tourists don't have time to hear. They can't get

a picture of that, can they? All those tiny pieces down
there in continual purification, a jig-sawed poetry
waiting to be put together again–tourists
at the top with cameras peering down,
then turning away, lenses misted, what's to photograph
here, anyway? They came to see a daredevil, or at least
a suicide–but nothing. It's what a friend said:
"Niagara Falls is just a bunch of water
that surprises itself by jumping off a cliff."

The casino, then, and afterward enough money left
over for admission to the two-headed goat museum
on Clifton Hill.

***

Tourists see the Falls as separate from themselves.
Tourists see the moon as separate from themselves.
Tourists see the wind as separate from themselves.
Tourists see the clouds as separate from themselves.
Tourists see river water as separate from themselves.
Tourists see gorge rock as separate from themselves.
Tourists see the trees as separate from themselves.
Tourists see the birds as separate from themselves.
Tourists see the waitress as separate from themselves.
Tourists see the man sweeping the floor
as separate from themselves.

***

We are all tourists here.
We are all tourists here.
We are all tourists here.

***

There is no feeling so desolate and beautiful
in a city struggling with its decline, than to stand
on Main Street as dusk gathers, a chill claiming the air,
to see the lights on in the laundromat, a man inside
folding sheets and blankets, a woman seated in the back
staring at a dryer as if it's a TV.

Next door is a closed neighborhood grocery, Slipkos,
really closed, boarded up for years, sign still
proclaiming "A Good Place to Shop."
Next to that a dollar store, doing straggler business.

In the laundromat, heat from the dryers,
the scent of spring flowers from the detergent,
chlorine trace, the thrumming of washers
going through their cycles. On the sidewalk
in front of the lighted windows, an empty bench,
facing the street, waiting for the parade.

It was a long pure note climbing, brass, that put two
men on that bench, then notes shifting
into a tune, a melody–
and one man is sitting, legs sprawled out, playing
a saxophone, while beside him, listening,

is the other man, an audience of one–
and everything breathes into that sax,
and is blown out, the dark street an avenue of music
from nightclubs that vanished years ago.

The saxophone is moving and reflecting beams of gold
from the streetlights, and I am standing across
the street, listening, and two cars go past
between us, windows tinted, tire hum blurring the
music for a moment, but he plays
on, music bathing the drunken shopping carts
on their sides in parking lots, old cars tarped
and rotting into the ground in back yards,
cars parked illegally, day after day
nervous in front of "No Parking" signs, crumbling brick
buildings, mortar sifting down,
telephone poles and electric wires–
and now only the man with the sax
remains, on his feet, sax down, sax up,
gleaming in streetlight glow and the stars
overhead, and the man in the laundromat
keeps folding clothes, shaking them out, folding slowly
as if in dream, where a man playing a saxophone
in the darkened street out front
is the most natural of things.

How else does a city find itself? You want the city
back, you gotta do that yousef. Calla cops,
is that an illegal parker, Charlie?
Where's at music coming from? You scared

to look at your river flowing, sparkling
with joy, and flowing power and greed
and sorrow, backdropping that sax, its long breath
eternally exhaling? Yeah, me, too.

So a man brings his saxophone to Main Street,
Niagara Falls, NY. He does not say,
you could grow up to be prez, young man.
He does not say no riffs, no electricity, no amps, no
watts, Ernie, no keys to that, Bobby, no scrap talk, no
trash talk. He plays:

And while he plays, I would have said, if someone
had been standing there on the sidewalk with me,
what you see is what you getz, man,
and that's the plan, Stan, but I am old and not cool.

And while he plays, a man pushing a hotdog cart
comes walking down the street. The cart has big
spoked wheels as from a bicycle, and a large umbrella
over it to keep night from falling on the hotdogs.
Now two of us are listening, but the hotdog man
does not stay long, because he has miles to go, etc.

So who was that man with the saxophone? Was he
a redman in the dewey night? Or a black man,
an ornate coal man hopping
a ride on a coal train, a fat head new man?
His initials are VJ, I found out later
when we talked, but I do not think he is related

to Etta, though it is possible he is related to Jesse.

When the night ended, someone could have shot
A cannonball down Main Street.
There were just the two of us, talking.

ONGUIAAHRA

I have lived here
and there in the lattice
of avenues, the streets,
and remember particular
years and seasons

(those times receding
into the funnel of the past,
leaving husks of themselves,

places, that visited
are found smaller than
their memories, half-known
in sunshine, curious
neighborhoods of summer
streetlight and dream

(the city, nocturnal,
jealous of itself,
sighted from:

2014 Virginia Avenue
2202 Michigan Avenue
2000 Tennessee Avenue
2952 McKoon Avenue
and 2965 Weston,
where I waited,
pretending indifference

but listened for its heavy
breathing in summer,
watched for its footprints
in the snow, grew
resolute, made plans:

track the city to its lair,
and drag it, kicking
and bitching, whining
and sulking, and promising
love and changing shape
into the daylight

I

Let us take time in our hands and rip
it apart to find out where we really are

Dawn has yet to come
night hangs over the house
awaiting the judgment of the sunrise

one half of the earth turns
in darkness and here in its dark
old thunder stumbles overhead
old thunder marches in the sky
the tired cavalry of old thunder
stumbles across the sky

shaking loose rain
the first singular drops
by wind against the windowpane
like an erratic tap
of fingertips, slapping
the leaves of the trees,
ringing a quick tempo
from dented garbage cans
beneath the window. (the empty cans
sing out with the touch of the rain
recalling all those corrugated
tin roof rains of yesteryear
and Hiyo Silver echoing through
Wurlitzer's cracking rain of static

and quick lightning photographs
the back yard already awash
and the wild poplar trees
in their wet posturings.

The rain pours down
for forty minutes, drumming hoofbeats
on the wooden sides of the clapboard house,
splashing at the stone foundation.
The house tosses like an ark
and as the rain tapers to tree-drip
I sleep, sleep.

At seven o'clock
am awake drinking coffee,

100

not looking outside but knowing
without looking that the day is tired
with gray cloud as no sun turns the beige
curtains on the east windows into gold. Today
I should look for work having been out of a job
for months running and now unemployment checks
finally running out also

but I step
through the front door
onto the porch

it's a soft day
a haze hanging and three
crows floating over the old
brown daguerreotype landscape
toward the civilization carved
remnants of Porter Woods and rain
is in the throats of the blackbirds
in the trees across the street.

Today I will not look for work,
the breathing of the day sounds
like rain. And around nine it does
no cloudburst, but steady rain,
rain falling the length of the street,
rain to the backs of the houses that sit
in a row facing my front window, rain

in the weed fields, and over the railroad

tracks rain, soaking the already damp
cinders through again.

The stores and houses, garages
and office buildings huddle together.
Rain is over the city, and even now
is falling, miles downriver, where
at gorgetop a shelf of rock thrusts
into the sweep of the rain

beyond and below it
the gulfing space
of the gorge

now shot silver
through with rain.

To the north the river
still flows dark and serpentine
to Lake Ontario, as when
I hunted past the place, walking
onto the jutting rock, body

in the mouth of the wind
and the hound's ears blowing back
close to their heads as they also
faced the weather.

(I have been where Father
Hennepin stood in the antique wind of 1678:

Four Leagues from the Cataract or Fall,
the River of St. Lawrence rushes with extraordinary
rapidity especially for two Leagues into Lake
Frontenac. There is a very fine Road,
very little Wood, and almost all
Prairies mingl'd with some Oaks and Firrs, on both
banks of the River, which are of a height that inspire
Fear when you look down, he said.

And almost three hundred years later
a friend of mine took a girl there (they lay
together in the grass and made love
in the thick green grasses of summer, he said.
And I too took a girl and a bottle of champagne
there one New Year's Eve, at midnight
listening to the small detonations
echo out there in the still space
and the far shrill piping
of thin factory whistles.

It was a new year. (The stars
remained fixed and constant
in their glitter.

Leaving, the girl tore a stocking
on a dead tree branch and thought me crazy

and jumping up through
taking the years like coming up

the back stairs two
or three at a time

I return home after years across country
and Army, to find highways and high fences
have wiped out the path to the rock.

But one night a new woman and I
reclaim the place, climbing
up from below, the proper way
of making that pilgrimage

the remark caused it
a half-casual promise
to go there
before the snow flies
before the snow flies.
Released, the familiar phrase walked
off and came full circle, trudging
back with the certainty of oath,
pushing us up to the rock

and the reach of space
was still there, as tangible
as its lower limits of earth.

Distance swallows
and we crouched down
up there on the edge
of the universe for a long while

cold wind flinging stray flecks
of rain in out of darkness

on the way down through worlds
of dim autumnal landscape
where it is always evening
where it is always raining

we are laughing
and our feet are swishing in the dry grasses
and the cool coin of the moon watches our descent.

On this day of rain,
sheet rain slanting
down the street, running off
the roof on all sides, making
a watery-walled cave of the front porch,

and I, not looking for work
sit drinking gin and quinine
evergreen soaking membrane and cell

and looking out
through the screen door
into the rain.

The door screen
bellies outward
like the gentle swell
of a woman just pregnant

and the rain hangs
in the gentle push of the screen

(it must be that children once lived here
shoving the screen into the shape it holds
in their eager straining to get out

and now moving down the street
through the rain, creeping along the walks
where rain is jumping, school
children in yellow slickers, unaware
of the past children who lived in this house
are walking home through the rain

it's raining
it's pouring
the old man
is snoring

rain, rain
go away
come again
some other day

as it did that other day
seventy-three years ago, two miles east
in a deep marshy woods
with a path running swift through
its hollows, and on that rainy morning
a young girl on her way

to school through the dripping woods
came upon a man who
had hung himself, turning slowly
in the rain, it was
as if he floated there in the rain,
she said later, a human question mark:

"why woods?
why rain?"

head at an odd angle,
watery face distorted into something
like surprise at the sodden stream
of his clothing, the constant

space of air beneath his feet,
that at last swung off the ground

"Keep both feet on the ground, Eli!
Keep both feet on the ground!" someone
had surely at one time told him

and at his toes pointing earthward
turning slowly first
one way, and then the other,

in pirouette,
with a grace he'd
never found in living.

A factory whistle
cuts the wet day in half
the clock stopped at 12:50
the second hand's endless
sweep made motionless
just past the two–
power lines must be down somewhere
in the rain, rain opposing those
horizontal lines not of its making

and it is good.

There is no time but the rain, beating
its multitudinous rhythms, dancing
on the rooftops, and in the street

II

When it rains
the river smell comes
into the city.

it is a question
of beginnings,
of what came first,
and of what remains

*in the beginning
was the ice, its river*

a sense of the river floats
through this place, old fissure
of icecap gorge deep in earth

the river where gorge walls
three hundred feet to the water
fall silent, holding solid
in mute gray, wan light
of paleolithic suns–
archaic shale beds slope
up at gorge sides,
groping slowly upward
through millennium
of shale drop

and industry also pushed up, cleaving
itself to power, above the falls, riverside
cumbersome, sprawling, surging up during darkness
up the buildings pressed huge monolith, grew
ancient in short time, windowbroken, grimed,
complexes–smokestacks, chemical tanks and process,
miles of conduit, plumbing strapped and wired
to outside walls, and electric the electric lights
shone miracle in the smoke that rides air,
the soot that settles.

This city is a place of boundaries
and dividing lines, each new piece
nailed on like rooms
to a squatter's shack,

tied together by railroad
rails, an old avenue
or a no-man's street
hanging loosely together
under the name of city

and the people in their rooms believe
they are the city, and see others
in ways rain cannot dissolve.

Rain does not erase
the boundaries and dividing lines,
it simply does not acknowledge them,
and falls irrespective of avenue
on everything alike:
earth, river, and city,
under the rain.

It is in the effect.
An old Italian on Pine Avenue
heaves up off his sidewalk bench
and goes inside, out of the rain,
to lean on one elbow on countertops
and smoke cheroots among the disgruntled groceries

his father
remembered Pine Avenue
as mud swamp, hummocks thick
with pine and down through
the middle, a narrow path of boards.

On Cudaback it is raining
washing down the stoops of ageless
ladies who look out of dull eyes
through clean windows into the rain

later in black babushkas, kneeling
in drizzle near the alley
at the back of the house
tying up tomato plants
fallen over in the wet.

And it is raining in Lewiston Heights
where a backyard party breaks up like a flock
of sparrows, scattering under the patio awning,
bright summer dresses wet, trays
of little three-cornered sandwiches made soggy.
Rain is falling in Lewiston Heights where
even money does not make it stay up

and below the ridge, in the town of Lewiston
where they are proud of their history,
the historical rain is falling

And the waters prevailed beyond measure
upon earth: and all the high mountains
under the whole heaven were covered

the river flows through the city
smelt are running in the sewers, pike,

blues and yellows, flop gasping out
of the flower beds

minnows flash down through the air,
tiny comets bouncing into the front lawns
where their iridescent sides
wink like new paper-clips
tossed into the grass

they slide headfirst down
the windowpanes and puddle
on the sill

and up through the thick watery branches
of big maples lining the street,
mossy sturgeon thrash

the river gorge rises on all sides
of the city, (where suspended
deep in secret stone
the shrill trumpet of mastodon
hangs quiet: with muddy clump

they shuffle parade-like
into extinction.
And held in dark walls,
the leather-winged flap
of great ungainly pterodactyls
drift ever off downriver.

It is dusk above, night between
the gorge walls sheen of water
faint beneath the husk of day,
and far below at the river's edge,
a wild duck's frightened cries
scrape the stone walls,
thin knives flashing

in the night rain
outside the pool hall
the windows steamed up
where the ghost of my Uncle Bill
paper bag tilted to mouth
inside the bag condensed
tears of vodka rain
down over Niagara.

In the daytime, like other places
out of the momentary light that floods

it is not the same:

a fat woman limps down the street,
choked bag of groceries in one arm,
and angles across, ignoring traffic

a dog barking some
where on a side street

a St Vincent de Paul store is on the corner

sad faded shade lamp in the window.

It is the reality of light. Walking home
on Portage Road at midnight, ghost Indians one
behind the other file overland, lower river
and Devil's Hole Massacre in unseeing
eyes silent moccasin feet on pavement
Catbird imitates police whistle.
The Indians vanish in
the headlights of passing cars.

On this carry-place I saw about two hundred
Indians, most of them belonging to the Six Nations,
busy in carrying packs of furs, chiefly
of deer and bears, over the carry-place.
An Indian has twenty pence for every pack
he carries over; and he dearly earns it,
for the distance is nearly three leagues. R.C. 1755

The city eludes me in the dark,
hiding between the lines of history books by day,
living in the lost voice of the deaf-mute handing out
leaflets with all the hand-signals, the American flag
and I AM A DEAF MUTE printed on them, reflected
in the eyes of the legless man on Falls Street
with pencils and tin cup

the city is more than
sidewalk and hundreds of feet
moving by

and the legless man knows it,
low enough to gain different perspectives,
to look up into its soft belly,
its secret places.

Home, in the darkened front room,
falling asleep on the couch, I hear
the skateboard of the legless man rolling
across the concrete face of the city.

I awaken to the sound of rain
again it is the incredible dawn,
catching trees against the sky,
and the patterns of rain in the street.

III

And where does the city
find itself

(printed

on the skin, spiraling
in the cochlea
drawn into nostrils,
lungs, in the camera
of the eye,

the play of light
on retina

It is not distinct from
I walk the streets
and assailed:

am haze of factory smoke hanging over the city
am raindrops sliding through the smoke
am city under ancient skies
am rain washing over the city
am streets, avenues, boulevards, alleys
am hiss of car tires in the wet streets
am drunkenness stumbling
by The Silver Dollar on Little 4th
am the first drop of rain on the sidewalk
am Good Friday living up to legend
am deserted bus-stops lonely in the rain
am seduction fumbling with trembling high-school girls
am the smell of rain out of the west

am torches weaving through narrow avenues during
the Festival of Lights celebration, 1929
am frog, an inert lump of pain on Grand Island, legs
kicking in a frying pan on Michigan Avenue
am turning on and flooding the city with laughter from
the top of Hyde Park Bridge, small pale face of NY
Central switchman looking up from below

am living in Center Court

am the sun going down in the Autolite dumps
am an ear listening to rain
am the ghost of Hyde Park Village
am paddling my canoe up Love Canal
am drizzle moving down from on high
am John Steadman escaping the Devil's Hole Massacre
am lost in Porter Woods
am rain soaking golfers, Niagara Falls Country Club
am spear fishermen of lower river
am three shopping days until Christmas
am rainstorms covering the east coast
am being stabbed 47 times on 8th Street and dying
in a telephone booth and no one knows why
am putting baby birds back in the nest and waiting
half a day for the mother to come back
am red blinker at Cleveland and 18th flashing out subtle
morse code messages that no one understands,
north. south. east. west.

am ice bridge breaking up at night, moving out unseen
am fear going over the Horseshoe Falls in barrels
am wind walking tightropes over the gorge
am raindrops dimpling Gill Creek
am colored lights changing on the cataracts
am the rumble of the falls all over the city
am crying in rm 12 of old Prospect House
am rained out game and loud talk in Stadium Grill
am backseat lovers in Starlite and Autoview Drive-ins
am calling my girl from phone atop of Seagrams Tower
am cool with convertible and sunglasses on Main Street

am sheets of rain moving down the highway

am perpetual early morning rainbow living in mist
at the Horseshoe Falls refusing to be photographed
am big yellow Euclid trucks growling
through the muddy and sleepy streets of town
am walking home in the dark
thinking sleep and tomorrow,
suddenly at the mercy of the Police K-9 Corps

am tourists buying souvenirs on Falls Street
am orgasm of all Niagara honeymooners
past, present, and future

am quiet in the graves in Oakwood Cemetery
am hillbilly music in downtown bars
am rain puddling on the sidewalks
am wash on the line flapping in the wind
am old age strolling around in parks
am popcorn dropped from the balcony in the movies
am mute American Falls dried up
by a dump truck, one bulldozer
am rain dripping between the houses
am watching endless Maid of the Mist
Parades for eternity
am accepting a pair of shoes from the Salvation Army

am making big money these days, talking tough
and drinking hard wearing steel construction helmet
am being periodically blown up in explosions

at Olin Mathieson felt ten miles away
am seeing the United Office Building as a headstone
marking the lonely grave of the city

am desire sitting in showrooms
am hope in used car lots
am settling in the mud, waiting for death in junkyards
am resurrection under the torch
am rain coming in the open windows
am walking around with a hard-on 24 hours a day
am shacking up in Griffin Manor
am late night Lehigh Valley locomotive chugging
am the specter of Sugar Street School
now on Hyde Park Boulevard
am according to the Chamber of Commerce an average
annual rainfall of 29.7 inches

am inhaling chlorine gas leaking out onto Buffalo
Avenue in the early summer evening
am the first suicide of the year
throwing myself off Luna Island
into the Bridal Veil Falls, body recovered
later in the day at the Maid of the Mist Boat Landing
am stark concrete power plant grafted onto the river
gorge a monstrous bee-hive full of ominous
late night humming

am bursting into tears on my 80th birthday
am crows cawing over the early Sunday morning city
am the single drop of rain hanging on telephone wires

am thunder living in the Cave of the Winds
am the last bleat of the last goat on Goat Island
am the Lonesome Elm
am bridges spanning the Niagara River
am the car horn that beeps once at 2 a.m.
am remembering the sudden thunderstorms of youth
am the LAST FREE INFORMATION booth
before Niagara Fails

am standing on a porch on 13th Street hearing a long
night freight go rumbling through; it is winter, there
are fires burning at the switches along the track
am delivering Sunday papers at 4:30 in the morning,
collecting money from dark tombs of empty milk boxes
am the river flowing morning noon and evening, night
and day, winter, summer, through past centuries
during this one and into the next
am raining all day
am raining all night
am raining on and off for three days
am hermit of 19th century Goat Island
still alive on 3rd Street
am the late late show
am teenage girl standing sideways in front of her mirror
am dying of boredom in Gluck Park
am taking trips on vanished old Scenic Gorge Railway
am fifty-third generation duck on Duck Island
am dreaming about the river flowing
clean and strong again,
the fish mysteriously coming back

and finally knowing
remembering myself

I am city
I am river
I am rain.

Part Four: Defying Death

CONDITION

The condition is one of balance
and in that way sways everything
buffeted by high winds
of uncertainty.

It walks the line on fingertips
on one side this,
the other that.

In tightrope walking
balance is enough (erect, head up,
the feet dancing securely on the wire,

but the instance
is rare and we look
for the plunge to one side
or the other.

A short history: (of balance

Blondin had it, gracefully from one end
of the line to the other, with top hat
and cane, with a man on his back, Blondin
had it. Spelterini had it, over the line
with baskets on her feet. Even Peer had
it once, but lost it.

We all have it, but seldom call on ourselves

for evidence. Policemen know the importance
of balance, and ask proof

insisting that poems
be written with the breath
and with the feet

the body prances in headlight
glare down the middle of the street
on the white line that extends
to the horizon, or eternity.

Let us remember, however, traffic
circles, intersections, right angle
turns, and other detours. Let us
not forget road construction
and other obstruction.

Let us re-enter nature in new ways.

The line runs
the open field, gossamer,
gleaming in sunlight,
a single strand turned

at field's edge, weaving a web
of language over the mundane
grass. The web balances
light and shadow, bouncing
sun back to the sky.

Balance is difficult To know it
leap guardrails, walk the gorge edge
where fields fall away, long grass
and broken rock underfoot. Let the sun

balance on the razor of the horizon
and in sinking, rise,
to morning sides
of the earth,

step carefully on thin dusk,
the river below, lights coming
on across the gorge.

To be home by supper time.
To grow up. Everything hanging
in the balance.

AFTER A LONG ILLNESS

We're standing around talking
how he suffered toward the end
how there was no need. Double
morphine drip someone says, turning
his wrists up, one in each arm.
Brompton's Cocktail someone else says.
So much depends, comes the objection,
on the doctors–who fear addiction
or who try to find that place
between no pain and a degree
of lucidity. Heavy rain is slanting
against the windows.
The last two comments:
Who needs it, the lucidity,
that is–and well, this area is
a hot spot, solid black on the map.
Then we drift off, cool, back
to work, ghost intravenous tubes
trailing after us.

KAYAKER TAKES PLUNGE AT NIAGARA

Down through
the rapids above the falls he
comes floating, kayak like a blunt
arrow, a twig, a hollow stick, him waist-
up from the center paddling, the white noise
of falling water thrashing the air. People
running along the shore as if in dream,
arms waving, tiny mouths shouting
without sound. He imagines cameras
pointing, himself on millions of television
screens around the world–gets hung up
on rocks, lifts himself heart thudding
awkwardly out, has legs again, pulls
the kayak clear, settles into it, shoots
forward toward the lip, paddle digging
water jumping to bare arms and chest, imagining
himself sailing clear, beyond the rocks, down,
down, triumphant–lifts the paddle
over his head, whirling it in salute
as he hits the edge, thinks
I'm going to make it! sees
the open maw of the gorge, mist, sunlight
on the far side, sees he's not sailing clear
realizes the weight of bad judgement
the error of imagination, tons
of water, heavier than shame.

ON MEETING KARL SOUCEK IN THE LIBRARY

We're heading toward one another
glancing down into the carpet pattern,
a repeated black squiggle over gray,
risky business, for me at least,
since it causes vertigo, nausea, makes me
want to fall into a chair, to read anything,
steady black lines of print that stand still.

When we look up, I recognize him
from his newspaper picture,
"Daredevil conquers Niagara,"
deep-set eyes, limp hair, parted
left, mustache, cleft chin–
and he sees that I recognize him, begins
to veer away, perhaps fearing that I'll
offer congratulations or ask for an autograph
and he won't know what to say–or because
he doesn't want to say anything–and I'm
veering, too, simultaneously, not wanting
an autograph, not wanting to congratulate him,
unless it's for making his way successfully
across the carpet.

Say what: Hey, nice trip over the Falls!
I really admired the way you fell and floated.
Can I buy you a beer? What
I want to know is, what's it

like wanting to die so much there's no fear,
but still refusing to take the Hemingway?
What do you think of Niagara,
otherwise? As a natural attraction,
I mean.

So I know what he's trying to avoid:
getting cornered in a bar where after
a few beers I'd be saying, I take risks
too, you know. I've smoked for nearly forty years,
I drive a little too fast for conditions
most of the time, I've told a woman I loved
her, and meant it, I walk through dark
parking lots alone, and when two or three
ease past me in the gloom I resist looking
over my shoulder which, my uncle told me
is the true test of courage.

But Soucek shouldn't have been concerned.
I wouldn't have said any of those things
even though most of them are true.
We pass one another. He leaves the library
and I get a book—one on daredevils, believe
it or not. To hell with primary sources,
especially when they slide away
over the wavering carpet ripples,
escaping to the street.

The next time I see his face
he's looking out from the front page, same

photo as when he'd gone over the Falls seven
months earlier: forehead's got that same cut,
his eyes look to the left as if he's seen
something approaching from that direction,
his mouth's open, caught in the middle
of speaking, a warning off, a snarl,
stay back. "Stunt kills daredevil Soucek,"
the headlines say boldly. He'd died from
a stunt gone bad, in the Houston Astrodome
where he was dropped 180 feet, in a barrel,
toward a tank of water, but missed, hitting
the tank's edge. He'd wanted the stunt
to be "as close to Niagara" as possible.

The drop at Niagara had been four feet lower,
but he'd lived through that one, had gone
to the library to read the scrawl of the carpet,
had seen something there: he wouldn't be
the Last of the Niagara Daredevils, his time
was limited, he shouldn't talk to strangers.
All those junk cars he'd catapulted over
had been hauled to scrap yards, he'd never glide
to the North Pole on that motorcycle as planned,
the Astrodome swam in a blur around his feet–
the Niagara ride had been his finest hour.

STEVE PEER
tightrope walker, Niagara Falls, 1878

Was a man about
of sorts who played
at cards at women talked
loud and drank too

much. Still he was
liked by everyone
but himself.

He was easily goaded
into taking a dare,
or buying a round.
He was, in short,
an ass, who felt good

with himself only once,
drunk, alone out over the gorge
on the three-quarter inch wire.

Ah–he was a flightless
bird out there, dancing
his drunken dance in
slippery leather shoes,
unbuttoned suit jacket
flapping awkwardly
in the night

and taking flight
leaving the wire, his last
earthly connection, vibrating,
humming in the wind, soared
for a moment, smiling

the lights of town
growing smaller
above him.

NIK WALLENDA WIRED
FOR ONE NIGHT STAND

For that walk across the brink
of the Horseshoe Falls and gorge
and why not (after asking for more
money just before the act),
in the 21st Century?

Let us count the ways: to Heaven
and to his fallen Grandfather there,
who died when he dropped from the wire,
to spotlights setting the mist-gorgeous night ablaze,
to his father, advising, encouraging him
during the walk, to the camera following
along on a wire of its own, to the ABC,
carrying his words to thousands at the site,
to millions around the world,
who watched on television,
listened on the radio and, of course, to the wire
upon which he walked, that tether dragging along
behind him, attached to his body harness.
Which he did not like.

If he'd slipped from that wire,
he'd have dangled there
in mid-air, a few feet below
it like a web-trapped insect,
antenna of balancing pole
askew, legs and arms akimbo,

until the rescue helicopter
in-waiting, whup-whup-whup,
gathered him up.

But he did not slip. Step by step,
we watched him go...the high drama of it,
in and out of the drenching mist, some of us
with the image of the falling Grandfather still
in our minds, 73 years old, out on the wire, feeble,
faltering, crooked smile on his face, wind flapping
his wide pant cuffs, equilibrium fading, sinking
to a knee in an effort to maintain balance,
toppling sideways, hand grabbing
the cable, but unable to hold,
falling, falling.

"If that had happened twenty years earlier,
he'd have been able to hold on," Nik had said
about that. There's a consolation for you–
that and the belief that he's "up there"
smiling down on Nik
and his high wire triumphs.

And so Nik emerges, step by step,
on the cable, out of the mist,
face streaming with water
more copious than tears, saying,
"I'm so blessed! Praise be to God!
Praise Jesus!"

Further on he says, about wearing the tether,
"I feel like a jack-o...jackass," the only misstep,
Then he's saying, "I'm strained. I'm drained.
My hands feel like they're going numb,"
all the time walking, heel to toe,
heel to toe.

As he approaches the Canadian mooring,
the cable takes a slight upward slant,
which he prefers over the downward
he'd walked starting out–and now,
nearing walk's end, he kneels,
smiling, pumps a fist,
and rising, takes longer steps,
normal walking steps, then
runs the last twenty feet
or so to the platform.

Now it is time for the skit
in which a Canadian Custom's official
asks him for his passport and to state
the purpose of his visit–
and he replies: "to inspire people"
around the world, and he's hugging
his family, and just as I am
remembering him saying,
during an interview,
that he'd rather describe
his performance on the wire
as "art," not a "stunt,"

he announces that next
he'll walk across the Grand
Canyon, and that the permits
are already in place.

ODE TO A PHOTOGRAPH
OF ANNIE EDSON TAYLOR

Soon the photograph will be a century old–
Not the postcard of Annie, unsmiling in high-collared
long black dress, hat a huge, dark mushroom balanced
atop her head, white handkerchief the size of an infant's
face bunched above her left breast, her right hand
resting on the barrel top about eye-level.
Although "Annie Edson Taylor, Heroine of Niagara
Falls, Oct 24, 1901," is painted over the staves
and hoops, the barrel's a reproduction–
her manager has stolen the original. She stands there
as is she knows it's a prop, as if promoting
something she doesn't quite understand.

The photograph of nine men and Annie is the one:
Below the Falls on the Canadian side of the river,
cascading water in the far background, Annie's
the focus of attention, walking a plank laid
between rocks to shore, helped by men who touch,
or who want to touch, hands offered in congratulation,
supplication, to touch a charm. She has no hat here,
standing on the plank, hair up in a bun, blouse
pulled from the front of her full dark skirt,
bent slightly forward at the waist. Below her feet
the water swirls, foaming, as thick as oil paint

Some of the men are dressed as if for a sporting event,
white collars, a tie, a derby, a casual fedora. Behind

her are two men–one with a walrus mustache has
placed both hands just above her waist, his gaze
directed toward the top of the gorge, heavenward;
the other's hands rest just below her waist as if to point
her in the right direction. To her left, standing
on a rock, a man holds her wrist with both hands.
Her right arm extends forward, fingertips nearly
touching the outstretched hand of the man
in the fedora, whose eyes are intently on her.

Other hands reach out in air, poised, in that fixed
moment that outlives the people in it: the man
with the walrus mustache is Carlisle Graham,
who shot the lower rapids in a barrel in 1886;
the man in the fedora is Red Hill, Sr., riverman,
who twice shot the lower rapids, who pulled 205
bodies, living and dead, from the Niagara.

But Annie's not stylishly dressed here, as were
those battle-ready Marines raising the flag on Iwo Jima,
but looking all of her sixty-three years, if not more,
befuddled, disheveled, waiting for her feet to take
small steps, as if she's being helped home by friends
after a night on the town, looking for all the world
as if she's just gone over the Falls in a barrel.

INSIDE STORIES, told me by a guy who was there, or knew someone who was

1

THE HISTORY BOOKS

Have it all wrong.
Take Annie, old Annie Edson
Taylor, who was a lush, and cadged

so many drinks in taverns
of the day that one barkeep,
(with handlebar and bar rag?
said "Annie, you'll haf to stop

botherin the customers. If you was famous
you wunt haf to ask fer a drink. Thed buy
thout you askin. Wynt you gover the falls

in a barrel?" and Annie said by Christ she
would, so tavern owners put up 84 cents each

to have the barrel built.
And that's not all. On the morning
of the event Annie changed
being a woman
her mind

but the two men who took her,

her bottle of scotch
and the barrel up the river
in a horse and buggy, stuffed

her in the barrel anyway
and cast her afloat.

They ran away to Buffalo, coming back
only when they learned she'd lived.

Returning to those same taverns,
she sold picture postcards of herself
and barrel for many years.

Out of such stuff heroines. Ah, Annie,
the picture of you being helped
over the rocks at the base of the falls,
will never be the same.

THE REASON

Bobby Leach got so busted up
spending six months in a hospital
after his plunge, involved

not only a bottle
but a regiment of them,
and two or three women
who hung on him sweetly
because they thought he
was about to die.

Helped into his barrel
by numb companions after
an all night party, he was kissed,
shoved out into the current, but
never strapped into
the barrel harness

and so caromed around loose
in there through the upper rapids
and over the Horseshoe Falls
feeling, as the story goes
no pain

(years later: a slip
on an orange peel, his

previously shattered leg
fragmenting again, blood
poisoning, death.

because we laugh, and drink
and dare, and are not properly
secured during the dangerous
times, the ground jumps

up and grabs the bravest
of us, when we least suspect
when we've both feet under us
out for a stroll on the boulevard.

FACT AND FICTION

I

*"Some things can be done as well as
others."* Sam Patch

Sam
Patch
was a
jumper

the first
daredevil of
Niagara

whose stunt
was to leap
from high places
into rivers.

In 1829 he
jumped 120
feet into
the lower
Niagara

then went to
Genesse Falls
where his

posters read:

HIGHER YET!
SAM PATCH'S
LAST JUMP!

And it was. They
pulled him out
in the spring
when the ice
melted. His

gravestone
reads:

SAM PATCH
1804-1829

II

Up there high
with only air in his
ears he kicks the ladder
back. It falls away, a demonstration

of gravity. Far below
horses gallop soundlessly, fires burn,
and fluttering like moths, faces look up
from under tiny hats. What is he

doing there it is better
than working in the mills

His heart a battering-
ram against his chest, he leaps
through the trembling air, believing
he is plunging into time, into the moat,
the river, to rise again renewed,
Indianhead penny safe in watch pocket of wet trousers.

BIOGRAPHY II

You hated the old dog
Rip "Old and smelly," you said
"just sleeps and eats."

And Rip, that last summer, just
kept following the shade through
the day, moving oblivious to hate

around the pear tree, heaving
to his feet as the edge of the sun
light caught up with him.

That summer lived out its span
the pears dropping overripe
to ground, where, under
the probe of wasps and blowflies
their flesh melted away, exposing
skeletal cores.

Rip also wasted in his
circular route, merging
into the shade he followed,
thin old dog stumbling
through the pears, until
the day his hind legs fell
out from under him
and slowly he dragged himself
out behind the shed to die,

I took the .22 rifle from
behind the door and went after him.
The shot made a noise not
even heard on the next farm.

That night after supper
you threw the pork chops bones
into the yard as always.

Two days later we look out
only the blackbirds and the bones
turning white in fall rains.

DEATH IN AMERICA

I come from a long line of hell raisers who
on a regular basis didn't
come home for supper

Dusk crept over the geraniums
on window sills, hot suppers congealed,
grew cold, the clock ticked
the wind blew, the barns
creaked and the chickens
fluttered in their sleep

while the old man was
out there someplace tying
one on, shoving the mill money
over the bar, getting oiled, blind,
loaded, mean staggering falling
down drunk

came crawling home when
they remembered home was there,
roaring about cold supper

The womenfolk trembled and wept
the kids got the Jumping H. Christ out
of the way before they got cuffed on
general principles, or stepped on
by accident. And finally, home,
the wicks turned down, flames

snuffed, the ritual
played out

it helped a man grab
the next day by the ass,
to live in a vast dark land,
next to the woods,
in early America.

Times when I can no longer ignore
the phantom woods at my back, land
stretching out in front, I turn
and crash into thickets of solitude,
let the pork chops and applesauce sit
until they become part of the plate

Need me a gallon jug of red wine,
a tall pale whore who doesn't
give a damn for no thing
or nobody, and doesn't give
a damn who knows it, with
eyes as cold and flat
as dimes

and the clock
stopped, until I remember it
and want it to go again.

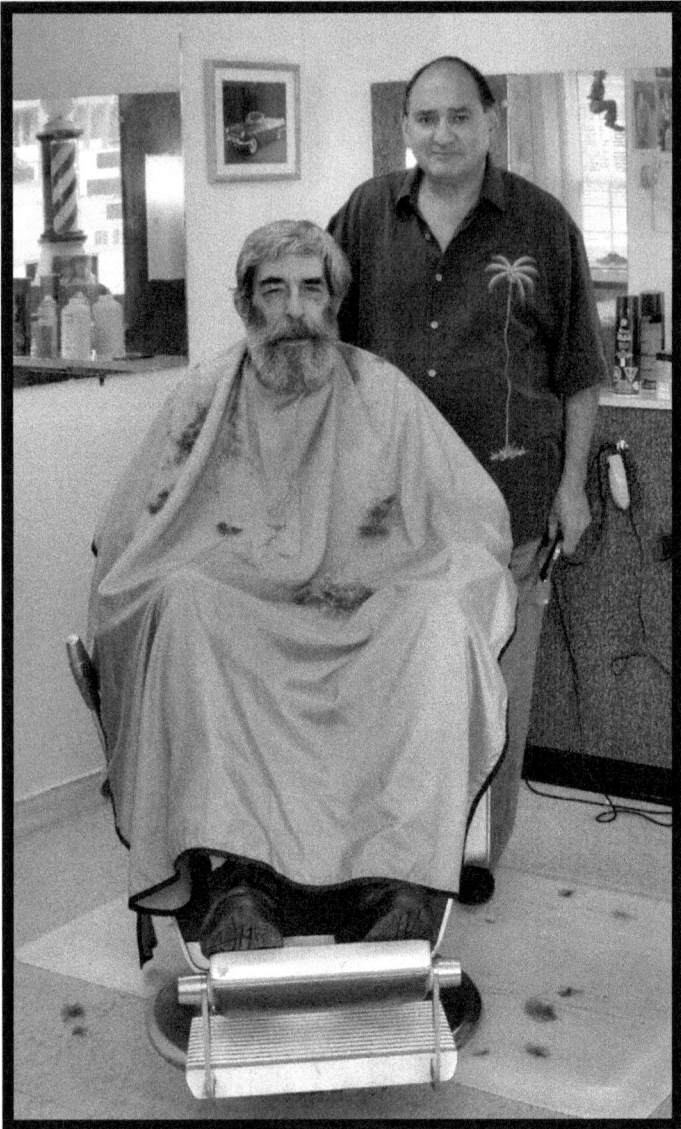

Photograph by Harry Brashear

GOD

God exists.
Make no mistake about that.
God is called by many different names,
just as a tree is called by many different names
in different cultures and languages around the world.
But God is not like a tree, because you can see a tree.

There are probably thousands of names for God.
It is forbidden to utter some of them aloud, or to even
try to pronounce them, and some are written in ways
to prevent this. When the name is written out in full,
it is also forbidden to destroy the name. Therefore,
the parchment, leaf, paper, etc, on which "God"
is written must be kept forever.

Now that you are in possession of this manuscript,
you must keep it forever. There were ways around
this prohibition, but I did not avail myself. I could have,
for example, written "G-d" every time I wanted to refer
to God. Then destroying these pages would have been
okay. But you probably have your own ideas about it.
Keep in mind that on most days, millions of people are
calling out to God, using hundreds of different names,
all floating and soaring to God in prayers, ritual
observances, and other entreaties,
but it makes no difference at all to God.
G-d doesn't answer to any of them.

It is a monumental understatement to say
I am not the first to take note of this. In a poem
by Kenneth Patchen, "The Reason for Skylarks,"
a very sorrowful event has befallen a giant
which caused him to do a terrible thing
and in an emotional state he

"Shook his fist at the sky and called
God a bitter name
But no answer came..."

So you cannot see God and God does not
respond to being called names. But God
can see you. God, of course, does not
want to be seen. Because God is "All Powerful,"
God could be visible if God wanted to be visible.
So God wants to see you, but does not want
to be seen by you. This makes God the Supreme
Voyeur, the Peeping God at the window of the world.
And God does not feel much like talking, either.

God is "All Knowing," too.
God knows the number of hairs on your head.
God knows the number of your days on earth.
God knows the number of birds that fly though the air.
God knows the number of fishes that swim in the sea.

God knows if you've been naughty.
God knows if you've been good.
But God has no opinion of either.

If you do not believe that, you must
have taken someone else's word for it
Maybe a prophet. How do you know
it wasn't a false prophet?

God is everywhere.
How could it be otherwise?
Did you think God was a Heaven stay-at-home?
Do you think God lives in the south of France,
or in Greece, or Rome, or in Pisgah, Ohio?
And goes to Florida in the winter
about the same time you do?
All of the above, actually.
Everywhere.

God sees the fall of the sparrow.
There is no evidence, however, that God
cares about the sparrow falling. There
are lots of them. Do you think God laughs?
Do you think God cries?
I don't think so.
That would make God too like a human.
God does not peep like a sparrow, either.
What does God do?

God exists.
That in itself is a lot of work.
If you do not think it is, try it yourself
sometime, imagining that the BLT's

and wedges of lemon meringue pie
will continue to be placed in front of you
for all of eternity. What is your question?
Do you want to know what God does for a living?

We have already established that God
does not laugh and God does not cry.
We can probably say God does not fart.
If these three things are true, then what
are those strange sounds you hear during a late-
night thunderstorm, between the lightning flashes?
And what's stinking the place up all the time?
What's wilting the flowers?

It appears God has a full time job getting
everyone's love, including yours. What God
wants with it is puzzling. It suggests God is not
"All Powerful." All God promises in return is eternal
life, via prophets, by the way, as if that's something
worth having. No guarantees, either.
Sounds like some commitment issue there.

Re: prophets. There are a lot of them, fifty-five
in the Bible. The Talmud lists the same number.
Some are men, some women. The Qur'an names
twenty-five prophets, after whose names, when they
are spoken aloud, it is required to say the phrase
"Peace be upon him," as a sign of respect. Often,
even when the names are written, the phrase
is abbreviated in parenthesis like this: (pbuh).

For the last-born of these, Mohammed (pbuh),
the word "prophet" is capitalized when referring
specifically to him. The Qur'an also says there
have been 124,000 prophets throughout history.
Naturally, that count stopped about 1400 years ago.

They were the PR people for God back in the day.
God talked to them and they passed the news of God's
existence and God's messages along to ordinary people.
How did they do? Well, you've heard of God
haven't you?

Me, too, and at a young age, at the Evangelical United
Brethren Church in the inner-city of Niagara Falls, NY
where I met God: a short, elderly man in a gray suit,
who seldom smiled and had jowls. Everyone hushed
when he entered the room. "You are in God's house
here," he said. This is my house."
His jowls shook as he spoke.
I did not know they were called jowls then.
That is one thing I learned in the House of God.

In Sunday School where the youngsters went
during the grownup's services, we had our lessons,
Jesus riding on a donkey, the Good Samaritan,
Noah and the Ark, and so on, and when it was over,
we joined hands and skipped around
and around a card table, in the middle
of which sat a model of a church, while singing
over and over "Good by-ee! Good bye-ee! Sunday

School is ov-er, and weee are go-ing home! Sun-day
School is ov-er and weee are going home!" We'd
release hands on the "Good bye-ees" to wave goodbye
to one another and imaginary people around the room.

Then we all would drop our grubby coins, pennies,
maybe a nickle, through a slot in the little church roof.
My sister thought she was giving her money to God.
I thought I was paying a ransom to go home.
That is another thing I learned in the House of God.
My sister and I had different ideas about money.
But she was younger, skipping around the table
with her short pigtails bobbing. What did she know?

My first haircut occurred in Bucky's Barbershop.
"Brush cut," my father said, "and make it short."
And out I went into the sunlight, a splash of Lucky
Tiger on my scalp that made me a grownup, skull
revealed under quarter-inch hair, the face in front
of my head grinning. In the surviving photographs
of that summer my face is open-eyed, full of faith,
a face not yet slapped or punched enough to be
smartened up. But I had been to Bucky's, where
religion was the New York Yankees, and God
was Joe DiMaggio, all the prophets looking
to the sky for signs of home runs,
RBI's, the World Series, the pennant.
Joe DiMaggio didn't have no jowls.

At the other House of God, in the basement

of the Evangelical United Brethren Church,
was a basketball court, where children
of members were sometimes permitted to play.
The ceiling was low, the floor, unvarnished boards
nailed over 2x4's. Jump shots were impossible,
all foul shots were two-handed attempts underhand
from between spread legs, a dribbled ball might not
return from its impact with a loose floorboard.
Dreams of basketball fame died there, while I learned
that God did not like jump shots, to have no faith
that a ball released to the floor will rise to hand
again, injustice can be redressed by underhanded
actions, and lay children do layups, layups, every time.

And the years passed.
The elderly man I had thought to be God died.
He had been a wealthy member of the congregation,
merely, which dwindled, and was finally gone.
All the hymns sung there faded. Remaining members
straggled out of the city to a new church each Sunday,
where the Evangelical United Brethren House of God
became extinct, taken in by the Methodists.
Being united was not enough to save them.

The building itself then housed the Niagara Falls
Little Theatre Group, where actors hit their marks
and declaimed. Did they perform The Crucible there?
Waiting for Godot? Was there a fake tree on stage?
Did ghosts come out of the walls to join the small
but enthusiastic audiences of family members

and friends and others who had continued to deny
that television exists? The casts got back into their
street clothes, wandered off to the sound of scattered
applause. Ghost hands passed through one another
making no sound.

The building struggled back, minus the circular
stained-glass window near the roof peak, stolen, sold,
or stoned to pieces by the neighborhood, to become,
as the sign across the front proclaims, the Higher
Ground Christian Center. The date carved in a stone
slab at building front is 1856, the same year the house
in which I now live was built far away on the Frontier.

Now I watch television to see cathedrals
of basketball courts, whose sweep of laser shows
could be seen from outer space,
whose ceilings soar high enough to threaten heaven,
whose gleaming floors seem paved with gold, where
chanting crowds cheer on their gods among those
who play the game, and it is ritual for one player
to scream at another, "You in my house now!"

What prophet prophesied the rise of the NBA?
Well, not one of them did, actually. Prophets did
not have that job. Their divine mission was to spread
the news of God's existence and God's word around
the world. And that they did, to millions.

The most people ever to attend an NFL game,

by contrast, was 112,376, and that was in 1994,
a preseason game between the Cowboys and the Oilers.
You even know who won that game? There you go.
And that wasn't even 25 years ago, let alone 2500.

Are there modern-day prophets? Yes.
Rumor has it they are mostly false ones.
What's left to prophesize about any more?
The end of the world? All someone
has to do is keep track of about 100
of them and when the world does not
end when they say it will–kill them.
The rest would disappear in a hurry.
They'd become weather forecasters.

Habakkuk, a minor Old Testament prophet
from about 612 BC, asked questions of God:
"Yahweh," he asked, "how long will I cry, and you
will not hear? I cry out to you 'Violence!' and you
will not save?" And then Habakkuk waited.

Time passed, though we cannot say how much.
We guess that it did, because he had more questions.
We imagine him there, day after day, playing his lyre
in the temple and praying, because it is believed he
was a temple musician. His questions may have been
incorporated into song or prayers. He may have walked
out of the temple at night, wrapped in his robes, earth
sifting between the soles of his feet and his sandals,
looking to the glitter of distant stars for answers.

Then, the scriptures tell, he asked more questions
of God: "Thou art of purer eyes than to behold evil,
and canst look on iniquity: wherefore lookest
thou upon them that deal treacherously,
and holdest thy tongue when the wicked
devoureth the man that is more righteous than he?"
It is clear a different translator has provided us these
questions. Among other things, shouldn't it be "who
deal"? And reading as hard as we can, speculation
is the closest we can come to determining
how well sarcasm survives translation
from one language to the next,
or whether it was there at all in the first place,
or inadvertently created by the translator,
or exists only in the mind of the reader.

But Habakkuk got his answers from God.
Perhaps the scent of sarcasm had gotten to God.
Or Habakkuk did not get answers from God.
You can make up your own mind about this.

How did God speak to a prophet? Did God's
voice come booming out of the air from nowhere
and everywhere at once? Were there witnesses?
Who did the transcription of these sometimes
detailed responses? The prophets or scribes?
Or did God "speak" to prophets by causing them
to have thoughts which they accepted on faith
were planted there by God? Scholars are at odds.

162

Either way, it is reported God answered thusly:
God would punish the evil-doers in God's time.
Be assured they would be dealt with harshly.
But not yet. This is a condensation, of course.

Habakkuk died satisfied, strong in his faith.
He wouldn't have asked the questions at all
of a God he did not believe existed. He wrote
the words of a poem, in which he reaffirmed
his faith that the answers he asked of God
would be forthcoming, but that he soared
on the wings of faith regardless.

The questions of Habakkuk
need to be resubmitted. The answers, this time,
need to be writ large against the sky, no prophets
or translators needed. God could do that.
And "Not yet" is unacceptable.

Not long ago I attended an Interfaith Symposium,
where the concept of God was to be discussed.
On stage, left to right, were seated a Hindu, a Jew,
a Christian, a Muslim, and a person of the Longhouse.
The seating was not alphabetical by faith, the first cause
of unrest for those who yearned for an ordered universe.

Starting at the left, they spoke about their ideas
of God: Vishnu, Lord, Yahweh, Allah, and all
 were knowledgeable and articulate and well-

versed in the scriptures, holy writings and traditions
of their beliefs. It should have been easy for those
in the audience to conclude they were all talking
about the same absent thing. The only butterfly
in the library was the Seneca woman, who said,
and here I paraphrase, with apologies for bad
memory and possible misunderstanding:

"We, the Haudenosaunee, or People of the
Longhouse, seldom speak of such a thing.
When we do, we refer to it as 'the mystery,'"
she said, making quotation marks in the air
with her fingers. It was impossible to tell
whether or not "the mystery" had capital
letters and because the Haudenosaunee
are oral cultures, we will never know.

So that is another mystery.
Put it on the list.
Do you have enough paper?
I doubt it.

What comes next
is a list of mysteries.
It's for a mature audience.
I wouldn't read it if I were you.
It's old stuff and an old argument
and you've heard it all and made your peace
with it, God's will, etc, so Peace Be Upon You.

You don't need to hear again about that boy, eight,
who died from cancer. His hospital room was full
of those brightly colored expensive toys and ribbons
and balloons and other things to make him cheerful,
and to make him live, but their magic failed along
with everything else, and when he died actually,
at the moment just after the doctor pronounced him,
and his mother gathered him up, his lifeless bald head
held against her, a weight, and her deep sobbing
could be heard at the other end of the hall at the nursing
station and her tears were not individual, but streaming,
dripping from her distorted face, flashing backward,
christening, baptism. God was there.

God is everywhere.
So where's the mystery?
God loves us all. God loves everything,
saints and sinners. It's all part of God's creation.
God loved the cancer as much as the boy, so
God just stood there, sat there, hovered there,
existed there, while the boy died. The ghosts
of unanswered prayers floated in the room.
Maybe God's mind was also on the sparrow
in the parking lot three blocks away.

So the mystery is how many tears
came out of that mother's eyes?
God would know. God would know the total amount
of liquid and the volume of a single tear and how to
do the math, instantly. Can the number of tears be

a measure of depth of sorrow? Are all tears shed?
God knows. What was the boy's name? Could it
be written here? Pronounced aloud? Should it?
It's all a mystery, isn't it?

Mysteries flash in the sun like machetes swinging
up, swinging down, for a few weeks in Rwanda,
1994, where multiple attackers assailed individual
victims simultaneously, hacking them to death.
This was more labor-intensive than gas chambers,
so much so that after a few hours the machete wielders
tired of their labors—and then cut the Achilles tendons
of those yet to be killed so they could not flee. Then
they rested, had lunch, a bottle of beer, before picking
up the machetes and taking up where they'd left off.
At first women and children were also slashed
to death, the women after being raped, often by gangs
of men. And then methodology shifted—the women
would be raped as before,
then mutilated, but not killed.
Their faces were slashed, hands severed,
arms, one or both, chopped off at the elbows.
They were told they were spared
so that they could "die of sadness."

How did such masses of people get assembled
in the first place? Once the killing started
in isolated but widespread locations,
those who wished to kill more of them
spread the word: come to the stadium

for protection, go to your church where you
will be safe from those who wish to harm you.
And they did come, by the hundreds, thousands–
and then the army of men with machetes would appear.

What happened then? Perhaps one of the men
with machetes would say, "Thank you all for
coming. You may be wondering why you've
been asked to gather here. Well, I'm going
to answer that question. Who's first?"
But probably not. It's more likely they fell
to the slaughtering like a horde of enraged
hyenas, and here I apologize to the hyenas
for my failure of imagination. No disrespect
to hyenas is intended. The screaming began.

God was there.
God hadn't seen so much blood in one place
since the guillotines in France. God saw the machetes
flashing in the sun, the blood streaming and spurting,
heard the screaming. the crying, the moaning.
Do you think any of those being butchered cried out,
"My Lord, why hast thou forsaken me?" Chances are
pretty good out of hundreds of thousands someone did.
Well, it wasn't the first time God heard that question.
You'd think that after almost 2000 years
God would have had an answer ready.

It was the 7th of April, 1994, when the Rwanda
genocide began and by mid-July, it was over,

an ethnic mass slaughter that mid-range
estimates, and it is horrible to quantify the dead
with this language, produced numbers
of the dead at 800,000.

That same year, on April the 20th, The Russian Dumas
declared that the Turks did, indeed, commit genocide
against the Armenians from 1915 to 1917.
On the 24th of April, 1994, President Clinton
issued a press release to commemorate
the tragedy of 1915 Armenia.
On the 27th of April, 1994, Israel officially condemned
the Armenian Genocide from the floor of the Knesset
describing it as "most certainly massacre and genocide,
something the world must remember."
It's widely accepted Israel knew
what it was talking about.

The word "genocide" was created by Raphael Lemkin
in 1943 to describe what the Turkish Republic
did to the Armenians. Even God did not
have a word for it prior to this which,
according to some religious legal scholars,
might be the basis for a defense.

The Young Turk Party had masterminded this atrocity.
"Young Turks" is a phrase that should never be used
light-heartedly in other contexts.
The German High Command remained silent,
though it knew about the mass killings.

They were taking notes.

Twenty countries recognize this as genocide.
By a single vote, 11 March, 2010, the Genocide
was recognized by the Swedish Parliament.
About eighty percent of Swedes do not believe
God exists. The Republic of Turkey rejects the idea
of this Armenian genocide. They have, in fact, passed
a law making it illegal in Turkey to claim that it
occurred. They are Genocide Deniers.
This is abbreviated "GD."
About ninety-five percent of Turks
believe that God exists.

Adolf Hitler once advanced an argument that the mass
killings of Jews would be an historical footnote
of little consequence. "Who," he asked,
"still speaks of the extermination of the Armenians?"
(He said this in German, of course–
which would have been, "Wer spricht immer noch
von der Ausrottung der Armenier?")
As it turns out, Adolf, millions
still speak of it. Even your words of scorn
have been written down and repeated.

Ways in which Armenians were exterminated have
been documented: they were worked to death as road
laborers, were casually shot, were executed in groups,
were burned to death, hacked to death with swords,
poisoned, were, the infants, dashed against walls,

were forced into death marches without food or water,
were bayoneted, were compelled to drag themselves
at the point of exhaustion far into deserts where they
were abandoned. They did not spend 40 years
wandering in this wilderness.
They began to die after four minutes,
four hours, four days, having lost all hope.

Some say the Armenian Genocide began on the 24th
of April, 1915, or the 7th, or the 6th, depending
on whether or not they are hair-splitters.
God does not offer an opinion about this.
Time means nothing to God.
What's a million years one way or the other to God?
That six days of work and one day of rest business
is just our attempt, via a prophet, to solve one
of the mysteries. I mean, come on, really,
how long did it take?

But it was April.
Ask Eliot. He may or may not have been influenced
by this. And the Armenians were Christian, the Turks
Muslim, and the mass killings had gone on years before
the turn of the century. A half million Armenians
perished. Many had escaped, fleeing
to other countries around the world.

I am bringing you a message from one of them,
word of mouth, from beyond the grave. He fled
Constantinople with his family in 1900. His name

was Hartan Bab Azadian. He was the Great Grandfather
of Debbie, who lives down the road from me
about a half mile. This is what he told her:
"The Turks were a lazy people. They were jealous
of the hard-working Armenians and that is why
they started to kill them." He was sure of this.
That's a good enough reason, isn't it?
Not to mention
they had a different name for God.

At the same time, compelling documents exist
that detail Armenians slaughtering the Turkish
in ways as horrible as were visited upon them,
men, women, children. Entire Turkish villages
disappeared, burned to ground level after the
residents were murdered. In one case a signed
affidavit tells how entire families were thrown
into a large well and then stones and boulders
toppled in after them. Is any of this true, do you
think? It would, after all, only be human nature,
would it not? Or is it disinformation? Does it
matter? It would take the Supreme Judge
of the Universe to sort it out.

Then the Holocaust. It is a word that stands for
behavior so horrific that it is a crime in fourteen
countries to deny that it happened. It is a word
that stands horribly grinning, holding hands with
genocide, extermination, Shoah, The Devouring.
It is a word that burns eternally, but is not consumed.

171

Eleven million died, about six million of them Jews,
and the rest Gypsies, the disabled, homosexuals,
Jehovah Witnesses, the "mentally defective," non-
Jewish Polish, that is, Christians, whose offense
was being Polish, all children of African-German
descent, and others who resisted.

One of the arguments that deniers make is that eleven
million, or six, or whatever you want to call it, is
flagrant exaggeration. It was closer to a few hundred
thousand at most. Well, then. That's a relief.
Even God couldn't complain about that.

Related to this, I'm poking around on line
and come across one of those "questions answered"
sites. The first one I click on has four questions.
Question number three is, " What is the relationship
between hitler and the Jews?" The "h" on Hitler is
not a capital letter. This suggests, should the answer
be pursued, that the relationship revealed might be
a dysfunctional one. I do not look further, having
quickly scanned question number four: "Why is
the bottlenose dolphin the state saltwater mammal
of Florida?" This is a low level mystery.

Then even words become corrupted, shrouded in horror
and death and unending sorrow–the words "final"
and "solution" cannot be together again, even the bright
crystal-like stars above combined with night summon
"Kristallnacht," where shards of broken glass glitter

on the darkened pavement, and all streets lead
to Auschwitz, Bergen-Belson, Buchenwald,
Treblinka–concentration, we say, concentration
camp, extermination camp, and as long as memory
flickers in the brain we see the gaunt figures standing
behind the wire, faces peering, eyes hollow, and yes
each of these had a name, and a family, and once
smiled in the sunshine and walked free on a sidewalk
and felt a fresh breeze blowing scents of spring–no
more, the old black and white newsreels, now in
documentaries, bulldozers pushing piles of naked
bodies into deep trenches, and the limbs in slow
flexing, flopping, a last embrace for the naked
stranger being shoved in the pile, waving a final
goodbye. There he goes, and she, your dead father,
your dead mother, sons and daughters, your uncle,
grandfather, your brother, sister, grandmother,
neighbors, friends, together in nakedness and death,
beyond embarrassment and fear and pain and caring.
It is the death that should shame us all.
It has been said God died in Auschwitz.

And we say, Never Forget. Never Again.
At least not to us. Another question surfaces as if
from a mass grave, a bone at a time. What is the
relationship between Pol Pot and the Cambodians?

Let it be known that Pol Pot, aka Soloth Sar, aka
"brother number one," together with his henchmen,
via the Khmer Rouge did murder, or hasten the death

of, between 1.7 and 2.5 million Cambodians in an
attempt to create a Utopia as he was directed to do
by "heaven." This is generally agreed to have begun
on the 17th of April, 1975, ending in 1979. The Khmer
Rouge targeted Buddhist Monks, the disabled, ethnic
Chinese, the educated, especially Western-educated,
of the Cambodian population. Up to 100,000 were
killed: beaten to death or buried alive in mass graves
victims were forced to dig for themselves.
These graves were called the Killing Fields.

Ninety-five percent of Cambodians are Buddhist.
That is to say that they do not believe God exists.
They do not even believe G-d exists. The idea is
irrelevant to them. This does not deter those who
do believe God exists. They know God exists
for Buddhists, too. The Buddhists just don't know
it yet. So God was watching this genocide,
also–keeping an eye on it, so to speak.

In the end, his idea of Utopia collapsed, Pol Pot
was under house arrest, bedridden, wheezing with
asthma, and suffering from face cancer, when he died,
on the 15th of April, 1998–the same day he learned
he was to be brought in front of an international
tribunal. He reportedly died from heart failure,
though suicide was suspected, or poisoning,
voluntary or not. He was cremated before
an autopsy could be performed.

Buddhists do not believe in the existence of God,
but they do believe in Karma. This will ensure that Pol
Pot will live again, many lives, perhaps 1.7 million
of them, one after the other, in each of which he will
marry twice, but his first wife will go insane
and die as she did this time, and he will suffer
from asthma and cancer of the face and die–
this may take eons, depending. Karma
is as oblivious to millions of years as God.

The two chief tourist attractions in Cambodia today:
1) the magnificent 12th century Angor Wat, literally
translated as "City Temple," once Hindu, now
Buddhist, and 2) the Killing Fields Museum,
where visitors can stare at 8,000
human skulls in a glass shrine.

In America, we have our own shrines. About a half
million people annually visit the Oklahoma City
National Memorial and Museum, located in the nation
about where its belly-button would be if it had one.
This exists as the indirect result of actions taken
by Timothy McVeigh, aka Darel Bridges, aka Robert
Kling, aka Tim Tuttle, aka the Wanderer, who was born
on the 23rd of April, 1968. Four days shy of his 27th
birthday, the 19th of April, 1995, he ignited the fuses
of a two and a half ton bomb of his own making.

The bomb was concealed in a rented Ryder truck.
The truck was parked at a curb in Oklahoma City.

The curb was in front of the Alfred P. Murrah
Federal Building. Then Timothy McVeigh began
to run. He had stayed in the Dreamland Motel nights
before. Unless it was the Grandview Plaza, room 26.
Unless this latter was a ruse.
Surely, he was dreaming.

Minutes later, the bomb exploded. It was so
powerful both of Timothy's feet came off the ground.
When he came back to earth, he kept running.
Behind him the Federal Building was demolished
in a jumble of exploded concrete and twisted steel,
and 324 other buildings had been destroyed
or damaged, as well. Inside the Federal Building
and nearby were the bodies of 168 dead, including
19 very young children who had been in the American
Kid's Day Care housed in the building, and three
women who had been pregnant.
He showed them.

This date was the same day in April as the Waco
Attack, for which McVeigh had been seeking revenge.
The people, the little kids and pregnant women
who died, had not been at Waco, of course.
It was also the same date in April as the Battle
of Lexington and Concord in 1775.
They hadn't been there, either.

McVeigh was apprehended, tried, and executed
by lethal injection in 2001. His act of terrorism was

thoroughly investigated by every agency you can
imagine and some that you cannot. In spite of this,
not all the questions were answered. Did he or did
he not have a microchip in his buttocks, put there
by the Army, as he claimed? Is that not a classic
symptom of paranoia, that is, if it weren't there?
Wasn't anyone curious? I mean, I am just saying.
With what did McVeigh light the fuses? Was it
a Bic lighter? Or was it a paper match, one of a book
of matches casually picked up at the Dreamland Motel?

And what about that leg found in the rubble
of the Federal Building that could not be matched
with a body? Were there more
than two other co-conspirators?
Conspiracy theories multiply as usual, as people try
to solve mysteries. I don't know anything
about conspiracy theories.
I just assume they are all true.

The name of the investigation was "OKBOMB."
The "OK" stood for "Oklahoma," obviously, but
the obvious was ignored, obviously. What was
okay about that bomb? If the investigators did
not think of that, what else did they miss?
Wouldn't "OC," for Oklahoma City have been
just as good for a name?

Ninety-five percent of people in the United States
believe that God exists. It is not clear if they love

God, but they believe that God exists. Perhaps
those occupying the Federal Building at the time
of the explosion were non-believers, or Buddhists.
But God saw the whole thing, saw it progress,
knew it was going to happen. God saw Timothy
mixing the ingredients for the bomb, saw the
sweat drip off his brow as he stirred and poured.

God knows if there were a microchip in Timothy's
ass. If there weren't a microchip, God knew that
Timothy was going around believing something
that wasn't true. God knows whether or not a paper
match from the Dreamland Motel was used to light
the fuses. Once, years ago, I stood outside with a friend
talking. It was summer. At our feet was an anthill half
the size of a basketball. All the ants were busy, coming
and going. Suddenly, nonchalantly, with one foot,
he stepped on it with all his weight and then kicked
it apart. I must have gotten a look on my face,
because he shrugged and said,
"Give 'em something to do."
When I think of certain things I feel
that look on my face again.

The statue of the woman is, from
the bare heel of her sandaled foot
to the top of her head, one hundred
and eleven feet and one inch tall.
She has a serious expression
on her face, befitting her role

of Liberty Enlightening the World, aka
The Statue of Liberty, aka Lady Liberty,
aka Mother of Exiles, and holds a torch
in her right hand, arm extended high
in the air. Her left hand holds a tablet
on which is inscribed, July 4, 1776.
This is in Roman numerals.
Declaration of Independence, we say,
Declaration Day, 4th of July fireworks.
Bombs bursting in air.

She faces southeast
toward the open ocean and,
therefore, did not see the aircraft
slamming into the Twin Towers
on the 11th of September, 2001.

The people visiting her that day
were able to turn their heads and did
witness that dramatic event, at least
the second of the two planes, the first
having drawn their attention. Some
of them, and others across the country,
came to feel that instead of the torch
being held aloft, her nine foot middle
finger should have been extended.

This is, of course, extreme.
The man who planned this attack
was already hiding in a cave with his God.

He believed God had blessed his actions,
so threats to bomb him back into the stone
age meant little to him. Did you take pleasure
imagining him scratching a hole in the sand
into which he defecated, warily looking over
his shoulder the whole time, and then scuffing
sand into the hole when he had finished?
But even so you have to admit he was not a dog
of the pet variety. These are led around on leashes
by people who pick up their deposits in plastic bags
as if they are nuggets of gold still warm from the day
of Creation. This was a wild dog who did his dirty
business and then ran slinking to a cave somewhere.

That cave was, we know these many years later,
very well appointed, running water, a flush toilet.
But he couldn't be found, it appeared, in this small
world that we keep hearing is getting smaller every day.
There should've been a microchip in his ass,
don't you think?

What most people don't know
is that his toilet did not flush with water.
It flushed with oil. We could imagine him
smiling faintly, thinking of the Western world sopping
up that oil at some time in the future, sieving it
and wringing out the sponges by hand
and using it to run our cars, to heat our homes,
to light our lamps against the gathering darkness.

We imagined him gloating over those he'd killed
and wanted to erase that faint smile with a bullet or two
in the right places, which is what happened–the face
that watched itself in old news clips, hiding, worrying
about the graying hair on its head, good bye-ee, good
by-ee, he was flying to his final cave, his ticket punched
and paid for by intelligence and SEALS who descended
from the dark sky, tapped him twice, and rose again
with his surprised carcass, and after the proper
words of his G-d spoken, dumped it into the blood
red sea, where ripples smoothed to conceal
his entry. He'd run, but couldn't hide
forever–and only God knows
where his remains are now.

His end was unfinished
business, but doesn't close this book.
Unlike the Mother of Exiles, we need
to look directly at the burning and collapsed
Twin Towers, where 2,992 people died,
including the 19 hijackers. According
to those sympathetic to the suicide pilots,
the smoke that rose to the sky that day
was incense pleasing to God.
Those murdered died horribly with time
to consider their ends, the ones who did
die instantly, were crushed and burned
so far beyond recognition that anthropologists
and archeologists have sifted though thousands of tons

of ashes and debris searching for a bone fragment,
something that could be identified by dna
as belonging to a victim.
And for this the families and loved ones prayed
to God. Some identifications were made
and some believed their prayers had been answered.
Now they could have this particle buried and have a
grave to visit, instead of the Fresh Kills Landfill
where the truckloads of debris had been dumped.

The tower fires had burned, raged,
and thousands of pages of paperwork,
blown from ruptured offices, fluttered
down blocks away, an obscene snow
of disjointed information explaining
nothing. Up to two hundred people
jumped from high tower windows
that day, choosing that death over
the roaring flames at their backs.
There was about ten seconds
to think on the way down. Perhaps
there were quick prayers for a miracle,
a soft landing, a series of awnings,
as in the movies, to break the impact
of the fall. The loyalty of keeping
the briefcase, now almost torn from
the hand by the rushing wind, should
be worth something, suit jacket open
and fluttering, tie streamering past
the face. God saw every last one

of them falling. God took notice.
Sparrows? God thought.
So many of them!

And this is why, children, the United
States went to war in Afghanistan. We
believed the Man in the Cave was hiding there,
and his friends refused to turn him over. As of now,
1,276 United States and coalition forces have died there
as well as 1,200 Afghan civilians. This is a total of
2,476, still short of the 2,992 who died
in the Twin Towers attack by 516.
But we need to factor in those who died
in the field in Shanksville, PA
and those at the Pentagon plane crash site.
Do you like heaping these numbers up and sorting them
into piles, comparing? Timothy McVeigh did.
He remarked, regarding his execution,
that one hundred and sixty-eight for one
was pretty good, or words to that effect.

And what did the Man in the Cave
think of all this? Why did he make
a plan to send our own planes to crash
into the Twin Towers, for example?

He had given us three answers.
I repeat them here and you can decide
if they are worth thousands of lives:
1) He believed The United States Military

should not have a presence, or be exerting
influence, in the country of his birth, Saudi Arabia.
2) He believed that Palestinians, who worship
the same God as he, are being persecuted–
killed and denied rights to their homeland by Israel.
The United States befriends Israel in word and deed,
with billions of dollars, and does not speak out against
the injustice. The United States persecutes
Palestinians by proxy. It is one of those
friends-of-my-enemy-are-my-enemy deals.
3) He believed Americans do not
properly love God, though 95%
of them believe that God exists.
He held up as evidence the idea
of "separation of God and State,"
a major tenet of the US government.
God should be running the government,
not the other way around, he said.

But most people in America
understand it quite the other way.
Even drill sergeants in the military know this.
They used to be fond of announcing
in loud voices to new recruits: "Well, men,
y'all better give your soul to God,
because your ass belongs to me!"

We might have asked Timothy
McVeigh about that. Part of his
agreement with the prosecution

to avoid further legal delays of his
execution was that his body would
not be autopsied, that he would be
cremated, his ashes spread in what's
commonly called an "undisclosed location."

And what is the relationship between
Israel and the Palestinians?
Well, they have had a long one.
I make no claim to understanding it.
I accept full blame for this lack of understanding.
Sometimes I do not understand yesterday.
Where did it go?

People, even gathered together by ethnic origins,
language, religion or shared misfortune, are not ants.
Not all Palestinians believe Israel has no right to exist.
But some do. Not all Israelis believe all Palestinians
need to be punished to reduce the threat of attacks.
But some do.

The Arab-Israeli War of 1948 caused
an exodus of thousands of Palestinian
civilians from the war zone who ended
up in refugee camps. There were about
three-quarters of a million of them.
Now they are a shadow nation, divided
among countries, scattered, over four
million, forbidden to go home again.
Babies born in the first few

years of the camps are now
over sixty years old.

That Arab-Israeli War of 1948 had
started before then, and although it's
over, it's not over. Israel and Palestine
keep at it, clutching one another in an
ugly dance–who does not know of it?

Military might belongs to Israel and the
Palestinians make bombs of themselves,
blowing up civilians, in buses, marketplaces,
stores, cars, checkpoints. Thousands go to meet God.
How they are greeted is unclear. They rise to meet God
with their shattered and burned bodies, pieces trailing
behind. Children die, women, men, on both sides.
Israel blows up schools, bridges, buildings believed
to be militant Palestinian headquarters,
water-treatment plants, all in the place
where Palestinians live. Civilians die.
The Palestinians fire rockets over the wall Israel
has built to protect itself.
They throw stones at the tanks. Israel bulldozes
Palestinian homes. Israelis called "settlers"
build yet more homes for themselves
in what is supposed to be Palestinian territory.
They invite tourists, and say, "Isn't the view lovely
from here?" Their own government condemns
their actions. They do not care. Palestinians
shoot more rockets. A cease fire is declared, one

of many. Peace talks commence, yet again.
Israel withdraws from a portion of Palestinian ground,
stops building there. Palestinians shoot rockets
up their asses as they leave. Israel bulldozes
more Palestinian homes.
I am reading about all of this.
The word "bulldozer" is starting to make me sick
to my stomach whenever I read it or hear it.
I am thinking of old newsreels.

I am thinking of the young woman crushed to death
by the bulldozer as it toppled Palestinian homes
into rubble and she attempted to defy it. Did she
think she was in Tiananmen Square in front
of the tank, forever immortalized? Did she,
at the last moment, slip? Do you remember
her name? Did God see her go down,
pressed into the mortar and sand
and stone forever stained?

The Committee For an Interventionist
God (CFIG) needs to increase its efforts.
God has not responded to their requests thus far.
God has not responded to their prayers thus far.
God hasn't even acknowledged the requests or prayers.
God is watching the Israel Palestinian tragedy continue.
God is just too G-d damned amused to intervene.
God is, after all, just too busy existing.
(We shouldn't presume to know the mind of God)
But these people just don't know how to love God.

I want to go back to that Interfaith Symposium
where, during the break, those who had questions
were invited to write them on 3x5 cards (provided)
and pass them up to the on-stage panel. My question
asked how the faithful of each religion were expected
to interact with the natural world, a harmless question,
really, easily answered–and it was, though what I knew
of the world told me the faithful
weren't in charge.

The Seneca woman said that from their perspective
all things in the natural world had spirits in them, all
to be respected–the animals, trees, the water, clouds,
the wind, even the stones, she said, cupping her hands
and making their shapes in the air. "We call them
the Old Ones." I could not see the capital letters,
but imagined them there. The Palestinians are
throwing Old Ones at the tanks.

I want to go back to the Interfaith and ask a new
question. I want a new card on which to print:
What's going on here?
Not merely between the Israelis and Palestinians,
though it's a good place to start, but everywhere
on earth. What's going on here? Thank you.
I'll take my answer off the air.

I have been to online sites where the Israeli Palestinian
tragedy is discussed, argued, cut into fine pieces, glued

together again with blood and hatred. I read for three
and a half hours, claims and counter claims, accusations
and opposing accusations, name calling, revisionist
histories of the 1948 War, the 1967 Six Day War,
terrorists anointed as freedom fighters on both sides,
Biblical scholars doing close-text readings
of the scriptures, pre-Biblical seers
listing archeological relics, right of return arguments,
remarks left by the passionate, dispassionate,
the logical and demented, colonialism is peace
arguments, truth seekers, the obsessed,
who have clearly made the issue their life's work,
some who have grown so weary of posting their
arguments to a world that may not exist beyond their
solitary late night tapping, that they no longer
have the time or energy to type out
the entire word "Palestinians," but have shortened
it to "pals," not even capitalized, which may
in itself be political symbolism or statement,
a floating twig of an occasional Gandhi devotee
swept away by the torrent, the angry,
the laments, tales from the displaced, ghosts,
the twisted and destroyed, the wounded, physically,
psychologically, and spiritually, a great weeping river
of sorrow unceasingly flowing.

I have learned everything.
I have learned nothing.

I remember part of a comment made by a local

newspaper columnist years ago: "Yasser Arafat
should take the tablecloth off his head ..."
and the end of the sentence floats away.
A schoolboy's insult. Nothing.
A drop of water in the river's flow.

But I can imagine circumstances
where I would kill him for it.
God could watch.

I have a suggestion for the Palestinians.
They should everywhere lay down their arms.
They should recognize that old truth: hatred
breeds hatred. Some know this already. There
is some mild evidence in the three line stanza
before this one. Then Palestinians everywhere,
men, women, children, in their occupied homeland,
in the camps, in all the countries around the world,
should voluntarily sew cloth badges to their clothing.
They should never be without them, from diaper to tee-
shirt, scarf, baseball cap, suit, burka, burial clothing.
These badges should be prominently located, of a size
to be visible from twenty paces. The letters "PAL"
should be on the badges in black. This would suggest
"Look at me. I'm a Palestinian.
I just want to be your pal.
Can't we all just get along?"

The background color should be yellow, the bright,
vibrant, florescent yellow of crime tapes.

Some may call the Palestinians copycats,
but these remarks should be ignored.
Of what could such people possibly be thinking?
In any event, a primary color cannot be patented, can it?
And who would sue them, anyway?

And when accusations and recognitions come,
and they will: "Hey, you're a Palestinian!"
there can only be one reply:
"I know you are, but what am I?"

When people all over the world, of all ethnic
backgrounds, colors, and religions
start wearing these badges, the battle will be won.
Note: God helps those who help themselves.

Because God exists,
and everywhere, too,
God was sailing along on those stinking little ships
that floated to North America. Of course God didn't
have to be sailing there, because God was already
in North America, watching those curious peoples
who believed everything had a spirit, the animals
God had created and named, the sunlight God
had caused to shine upon them, everything.
Didn't they understand it's all about Dominion?
The closest they had come to loving God
was thinking God was a "mystery," perhaps
a Sacred Mystery. Well, they had a lot to learn.
God would show them what smallpox and guns

were all about. God would give them a mystery.

There were already millions of people
already living "here," that is to say in what
came to be called the United States and Canada,
when the little ships tossed anchors and those
aboard began to yell "We've discovered a new land!"
New to them, maybe. But God had known it was here
all along. And so did the estimated twelve million
"Indians" who were living here. It was old news
to them, the woods, the mountains, the plains,
the old neighborhood, home.
As it came to pass, not long after that, say
several hundred years or so, almost nothing
in God's time, over 200 of these tribes were gone,
evaporated, had ceased to exist. They were extinct.
They would never return. Most often, their languages
were gone also, not a word remained. Expressions
for the things of this world, gone. Their creation stories,
gone. Their art, gone. The tattoos on their bodies, gone.
Their clothing and dwellings and tools and spiritual
visions, gone. Their distinctive faces gone.
Humor gone. Tears gone. Joys gone.
Laughter gone. Their individual names gone.

The names of the tribes gone, really, because the
remnants left to us were recorded in Spanish,
French, English, or other language
not their own, so we are playing a "sounded like"

game here, centuries old. But some are listed here,
nevertheless, these smudged echoes left behind,
so that they may be seen and spoken
aloud once more in the world.
It's up to you, gentle reader.

Acuera, Accohanoc, Adi, Alughquaga, Arawaks,
Arkokisa, Aroyel, Atakapa, Attikamigues, Bayogoula,
Beothuks, Cape Fear Indians, Chatot, Chawasha,
Colapissa, Congaree, Coosa, Gaquagaono
(Eries),Huma, Juaneno, Quaqua, Quinaiveelt,
Karankawa, Kaskaskia, Koyeti, Mascouten, Muskogee,
Nipuics, Onguia:hra (the Neutrals), Opelousa, Patuxet,
Pawtuckets, Palaches, Pedee, Pennacook, Pulacuam,
Pamlico, Purupuru, Santaa, Sewee, Shakori,
Sissipahaw, Sugeree, Susquehannock, Taensa,
Tangipahoa, Tawasa, Timucua, Tionontati, Tonkawa,
Waccamaw, Washa, Winyah, Wappinger, Waterees,
Wampanoag, Yaquina, Yahi-Yani, Yamel, Yaquina,
Yazoos, Yonkalla, Yustaga

If you have merely scanned these names,
that is not good enough.
You need to sound them out loud, even in a whisper,
to bring them into the world again.
Light a candle, burn a little tobacco.
Try again. Get a cup of coffee or tea. Smoke a cigarette.
God did not seem to much notice their passing.
You can do better than that.

Of course you will want to know
some of the details of what God did to the "Indians."
It isn't always the Devil that is in the details.
I am not happy to tell you,
and those men who did it are not to be excused.
We are just trying to get to First Causes here.
If men are given the capacity to choose cruelty and evil,
and they do so, then the least that can be said in a quiet
voice is these men did not love God.
Not enough, anyway.
And they weren't God-fearing enough, either.

A few details: In sunny California, 1853, the Yreka
Herald published an appeal to the government
for funds to pay "citizens...to carry on a war
of extermination until the last redskin
of these tribes has been killed." Two years prior
the Governor had promised that "a war of extermination
will continue to be waged between the two races until
the 'Indian' race becomes extinct." In 1855, Shasta City
offered a bounty for severed "Indian" heads,
five dollars each.
A resident left written testimony that he witnessed
mules being led into town, each carrying eight to twelve
heads. The town of Honey Lake, eight years later, paid
25 cents each for scalps. California paid one million
dollars two years in a row for militias to hunt down
and slaughter "Indians," men, women, children, infants.
God did not save them. After the first year, the State
evidently felt it was money well spent. God saw

those heads tied to the jug-headed mules.
Were they in sacks, lashed on?
Were they proudly dumped in
the dusty street in front of Town Hall?
Was the bounty payment in gold?
The gold rush was on.
That gold is probably
still in circulation.
People don't
throw gold
away.

The militias went about their business
with extreme prejudice, killing not only
the warriors, but the elderly, men, women,
and children, a phrase too easily spoken,
too common these days, to mean much.
But descriptions of the day tell
of youngsters scarcely old enough
to walk, crying, attempting to flee,
stabbed down with bayonets, clubbed,
swung by their heels into the ground,
smashing their fragile skulls, mothers
slashed, stabbed, shot and clubbed
to death, infants torn from their wrappings
and killed. There was, of course, some mercy,
as well, mixed in with the slaughtering, which
was that they were all killed. The fear and anguish
and suffering and sorrow was of brief duration.
There was no grief.

There were none left to mourn.
Perhaps God had planned it that way.

Do you remember that giant who shook
his fist at the sky and called God a bitter name?
I want to know what bitter name it was. This all
happened a long, long time ago, even before your
childhood, when giants roamed the earth and ordinary
people thought nothing of it. Magic beanstalks grew all
the way to heaven, or almost there, above the clouds.
There were trees of children then, where a mother
could gently pluck a child and take it home to love.
This was called The Tree Of Life.

A lot has changed since those days.
The giants are gone, extinct, by all
accounts, and the magic beans seem
to have also disappeared. This is just
as well, since the stalks would be growing
into the flight lines of aircraft in these modern
times. Mothers now grow babies inside their
bodies as had those mothers whose children
were slain by the militias. I had an Uncle once
who cursed. He did this rarely, but when he did,
one unclenched hand would shoot
into the air and he would exclaim:
"Shit a God damn!"
It was the most vile thing he could imagine.

The name shouted into the sky by the giant

is lost to us now. His language is gone.
But I still want to know what it was.

So whatever happened to The Tree of Life?
It had a fall from grace, lost its capital letters,
stayed a living tree, anyway. Deep in some
vegetative memory folded in the rings
that measured years backward, beyond
the seed to all the trees before, were
the codes for when its ancestors grew
human babies, when it was worshiped,
the Druids chanting, when its slow language
was understood by the two-legged ones.
The tree of life awakened to find itself
hiding in the American elm, once glorious
across the continent, now everywhere
dying with the incurable Dutch elm disease.
God knows it was trying to hang on.
Once it had made green summer tunnels
of small town streets across America,
tough branch ends gripped by the suspended
woven nests of Baltimore Orioles, hanging
like warm gray hearts.

Perhaps now you are thinking that God is like a tree.
Oh, yeah? Perhaps you are thinking of the Survivor
Elm, which is part of the Oklahoma City National
Memorial. The tree is about 100 years old now.
It has gotten its capital letters back. It was torn
and broken by the blast, partially burned.

And then it sprouted new growth, one sprout,
two, and people leapt to help and today
the tree lives in memorium, its seeds
gathered, new trees started, distributed
all over the country for other memorials
and school-yards and gardens, each
carrying susceptibility to the Dutch elm
disease. Here! One for you! And you!
These young trees will probably never
reach maturity, but while they live:
a memorial, lest we forget.

Other trees have joined the Survivor Elm
nearby: The Amur Maple, native to northern
Asia, China, Japan, Manchuria; the Bosque
Elm, China, which has shown "resistance"
to the disease; the Chinese Pistache;
the Oklahoma Redbud. Perhaps
they are murmuring together now,
about things they understand
and things that they do not:
The Trail of Tears
The Bataan Death March
Hiroshima, Nagasaki,
The Rape of Nanking,
the slumber time of winter,
laughing children, sunshine.

There are empty chairs at the National

Memorial, too, one for each of those
who died there, and a reflecting pool,
where a thin sheet of water flows,
over a surface of polished
black granite. Visitors are invited
to look into the pool to see the reflections
of their faces, forever "changed by domestic
terrorism." Better to look for the face of God
reflected there from high among the scudding
clouds than to merely seek the image
of your own mysterious face.

Speaking of domestic terrorism:
Nunna daul Isunyi
which, translated from Cherokee
to English, means
Trail Where We Cried, or
a variation: Nunahi-duna-dlo-hilu-i
Trail Where They Cried
and one more remove
to get people out of it:
The Trail of Tears.

This story has been told many times.
It has been written on talking leaves,
as will be done here, and sung
with Bitter Tears, as bitter
as that name the giant
called God.

The decider here: Andrew Jackson.
He has been called the exterminator.
He was, as we say, guilty as hell.
But he'd had a rough early life.
His father died the year he was born.
His mother died fourteen years later.
His two brothers died in the Revolutionary War.
Captured by the British, he refused to polish
the boots of an Officer, who struck at him
with a sword, slashing his hand to the bone.
He fought in up to a dozen duels. He shot
and killed Charles Dickinson in a duel.
He'd allowed Dickinson to shoot first
and was hit in the chest. He carried
a musket ball in a lung close to his heart,
occasionally coughing up blood,
until he died, thirty-nine years later.
He owned up to 150 slaves. He fought
the Creek "Indians" at Horseshoe Bend, 1814.
He fought in the 1st Seminole War, 1817-1819.
His nickname was to become "Old Hickory."
He was Scots-Irish, Druid ancestors likely.
He became the 7th President of the United States.
He survived an assassination attempt when
his assailant's pistol misfired as did a second
pistol the man then pulled out. The firearms
were examined and found to be in perfect working
order. Their failure to discharge was attributed
by many to Divine Providence, that is to say: God.

As a former "Indian" fighter he defied the Supreme
Court and forced 15,000 Cherokees from Georgia
on an 800 mile march to what is now Oklahoma,
along with Choctaw, Creek, Seminole, and others.
Gold had been discovered in Georgia.
Two thousand died on this 1838-39 march.
Jackson himself died six years afterward.

He was a great man, though flawed, with a left
eyebrow which appears grown old before its time.
His face is now on the twenty-dollar bill.
On the reverse side are the words
"IN GOD WE TRUST" floating
over the White House.
These four words
were added in 1963.

History shuffles along its twisting trail
and so it is with the Trail of Tears,
2,200 miles winding through nine states,
land and water, bearing witness, like God,
to the tribes who walked them with lost feet.
Shepherded by Federal troops and state militias
they died slowly alongside and in the camps.
They'd been promised food and blankets,
neither of which came in sufficient quantities.
It was winter. To boost morale, the Cherokee
sang Amazing Grace during the journey, in their
own language. But some tribe members, promised

new land, had gone willingly. They sang, too.
Moses had led the slaves out of bondage
in a 40 year journey to the Promised Land.
Slaves in America fled their owners to join
the Seminoles and fight the settlers. The wealthy
of the Cherokee owned about 2000 black slaves.
Moses was the only prophet, it has been said,
who gazed upon God's face, which is much
preferred to searching for a wavering image
in a reflecting pool. He left no sketch behind.

Disagreement still exists, but it is widely
accepted that 4,000 tribe members died,
though some estimates are much higher.
Perhaps we can agree that one death
per half mile is a reasonable estimate.
In 1987, the US Congress designated
The Trail of Tears National Historic Trail.
God, of course, was present at the ceremony.

One hundred and three years after the Trail
of Tears journey ended, if you believe
such journeys end, on the 10th of April,
another forced march began:
The Bataan Death March, aka
The Death March of Bataan, aka,
Batan Shi no Koshin, in Japanese.
Which do you prefer? Can the death
toll be reduced by making the right choice?

Prisoners of war, having surrendered
to the Japanese the day before, started
a 70 mile forced march, about 70,000
of them, Americans and Filipinos. They
had been promised humane treatment.
"We are not barbarians," the Japanese
Aide de Camp told the surrendering Officer.

So off they went in the tropical heat,
all 70,000 of them, though some sources
say 76,000, sick, hungry, malnourished
from the long battle leading to their surrendering,
stretched out along the road, a grotesque parade
taking their first steps of the 70 mile journey
to the prison camp, though some sources say
it was sixty miles. There were, by any account,
a lot of them, and they had a long way to go.

Many were to have their long walk shortened
by their captors. Those who requested water
were shot to death without hesitation.
Those who stumbled and fell were shot.
Those who attempted to escape, shot.
Some of the fallen were purposefully run
over by trucks accompanying the convey.
Those who attempted to help a fallen
comrade were also shot, others bayoneted,
beheaded, disemboweled, beaten to death
with rifle butts. Thirty of the men broke ranks
to crowd around a water source at roadside.

The Japanese soldiers set up machine guns
and killed them all. Soldiers in jeeps extended
bayonets to cut the throats in lines of captives
as they drove past. Those behind, eyes turned
aside, had to keep moving, around and past
their throat-slit companions, sprawled in the hot
road, limbs twitching, gushing blood, bleeding out.
These executions would have been more brutal
had the Japanese been barbarians, of course.

About 54,000 completed the march. More died
in the camp as a result of their ordeal and the poor
treatment they received there. General Masaharu
Homma had been in charge of the Philippine
campaign, and had, after the war, gone home
to a quiet life. Though he was not directly
involved in the Bataan Death March, he
was deemed responsible, extradited,
tried for war crimes, a phrase some find
a redundancy of the first order, found
guilty, and executed on 2 April 1945.

In some ways Homma had been a merciful leader.
His wife had appealed directly to President Eisenhower
to spare his life. This appeal was, obviously, denied.
To die by hanging would have been an insult.
He was killed by firing squad in the Philippines.
Somebody had to die for that shit.

At the annual reunion of the remaining survivors

of The Bataan Death March, in San Antonio, Texas,
two days shy of April, the Japanese Ambassador
to the United States, Ichiro Fujisaki, formally
apologized, on Memorial Day, 30 May 2009
for the behavior of his government 64 years before.

Note: the United States had been invited
into the War at Pearl Harbor, where 2,350 died.
The War ended with the dropping of atomic bombs
on Hiroshima and Nagasaki, where 196,000 died.
These bombs had names: Little Boy and Fat Man,
respectively. Most of those who died were civilians.
They were crushed, burned horribly, vaporized,
no particles left to retrieve for burial.
The 196,000 is the high-end estimate,
but later estimates seem to embrace it,
projecting to 200,000 the number of deaths
from the bomb drops in 1945 to 1950,
from radiation sickness and related illnesses.

These civilians had not been
at Pearl Harbor or at Bataan.
Eye-for-an-eye admonishments
do not pertain in wartime.
Timothy McVeigh hadn't yet been born,
but we were giving him a history lesson.

Currently, the central faith in Japan
is a combination of Shinto, Buddhism,
and folk superstitions, of many sects,

hundreds of them, called the New Religion.
God does not exist for 64% of Japanese.
God does exist, this means, for 36%.
Is the ratio somewhat of a mystery?
What was it before the bombs?

We revisit the man in his so-called cave
with his flush toilet, who believed God
should be in charge of governments.
God can't even run church governments:
during The Reformation, the Christians
almost tore off their own heads in long
theological disputes over matters
such as the right to read God's Word
in the Bible for themselves, to have it
translated out of Latin and into English,
French, German, and other languages,
such as whether or not the actual body
of Christ was present in the wafers
used in Communion, or whether baptizing
infants was a sufficient entry into the faith.
How could infants be aware of anything?
A second baptism would be required
when they were old enough to love God.

These examples are oversimplification
in the extreme. You are handed an acorn
and a leaf, to understand the tree in all
its spreading, branching, and root journeys.
The issues might seem trivial at such remove.

But know that French Wars of Religion lasted
for a century plus 31 years, that tens of thousands
died in Europe as Protestant congregations grew
and challenged the authority of the Catholic Church,
that clergymen were burned at the stake for refusing
to accept bread was the literal flesh of Christ, that they
died in front of crowds and their own families,
consumed by the flames without screaming
in pain, often, as documented, beating
their chests with charred stumps
where hands had been, proclaiming
love of God and exhorting their flocks
to remain faithful. There were many of them.
The smoke from those fires still swirls, drifts.
Their descendants walk among us today.

Anabaptists and Huguenots suffered the most.
The Anabaptists, who believed a second baptism
to be required, were declared heretics by the Roman
Catholic Church, and executed by drowning, as lay-
people joked they were being given a third baptism.
The Huguenots, French Protestants, rose up in France
after Martin Luther, were also persecuted by the
Catholic Church. They opposed the rigid dogma
of the Church in favor of a more personal
relationship with God. Power struggles ensued.
The Huguenots were two million strong in France
in the mid-fifteen hundreds. Catholics, sixteen million.

In the St. Bartholomew's Day Massacre of 1572,

that lasted for weeks, spreading into the countryside, up to 70,000 Huguenots were put to death, 25,000 in Paris. This slaughter was condemned by Pope John Paul in 1997. This is a good example of better late than.

The exodus of the Huguenot, which would end up at about a million, had begun before this, around the world, to North America, where Catholic persecution followed. In 1565 in St. Augustine, Florida, between 300 and 350 Huguenots were slaughtered by sword, by the order of Catholic Pedro Menendez of Spain, acting on behalf of his King. The Huguenot had surrendered and their hands had been tied. They had surrendered "unconditionally" and so could not complain that protocol had been broken. Menendez said he was "chastising them" to serve "God our Lord." He did well and we hope he got his just reward. It was the ultimate chastisement. They probably served God a lot better after that. God was silent.

About 400 years later, descendants of the Huguenot were widely spread. They were aware of their history and knew how their fore bearers had suffered. They were active in many Protestant faiths.

And so it came to be that in the summer of 1937, in Quebec, Canada, up in the woods about 100 miles north of Montreal,

a Catholic Priest was walking toward a little cabin.
The Priest could have been from a parish in St. Donat,
the nearby village, or from St. Agathe, or St. Jerome,
or St. Jovite all evidence of early Catholic settlement
persisting until the present, with over 85%
of the inhabitants Catholic.
They are the French speaking French-Canadians.

The Priest didn't know he was approaching the cabin
of the Lefrancois family, French-Canadian Protestants.
He tapped on the door and Mrs. Lefrancois opened it.
Perhaps they exchanged pleasantries. She did not invite
him inside. Then her daughter, an only child, about five
years old, appeared beside her, clinging to her long
apron, looking up at the Priest. "Oh," the Priest said,
"elle va faire une belle religieuse, quand elle grandit!"
In English this is:
"Oh, she'll be a lovely nun when she grows up!"
Mrs. Lefrancois' reply: "Au cours de mon cadavre!"
In English this is: "Over my dead body!"
She closed the door.
As it closed, she probably said, "Au revoir"
and we all know what that means.

God, present everywhere, witnessed this.
There's no proof. God did not kill the Priest.
God did not burn the cabin with the mother
and child inside. The little girl grew up and married me
and we had forty years together before she died.
God was present when she died.

You think not?
Remember the sparrow.
Charles Lamb was there, too.
And I was.

Charles Lamb: what could I tell you about him?
He is a Sierra Club member–has been for years.
He could have answered the first question
I'd asked at the Interfaith Symposium that day,
and answered it well. He'd been there, but we'd
arrived separately, surprised to see one another.
He is tall, somewhat thin, with white hair and beard.
He is older than the State of Israel. His whole face
radiates goodness, which will follow him all the days
of his life, an openness, peacefulness, faith.
He is a man of God, a Reverend.
God is G-d damned lucky to have him.
Charles probably believes that's reversed.

He once wrote a letter to the President
of the United States, cosigned by seven others
from religious communities, asking the President,
a self-described Christian, to put an end to secret
prisons and the torture of detainees. This was post
Abu Ghraib. It quoted passages from the Bible.
The letter went out like an unanswered prayer.

There are still men scurrying about here, clutching
fading documents and reports, largely forgotten,
secretly praying each night to God that WMD's

will be discovered soon. In Iraq, that is.
When I was a young kite-flying kid,
we used to write notes to God and thread
them onto the kite string where the wind
would carry them up, up to God, beyond
where we could see them, or at least as high
as the kite. I forget what we wrote on those little
scraps of paper. Those scurrying men, as high
as kites, which almost everyone knew from the start,
on TV displaying sketches of imaginary bio-trucks
and vials of baking soda and telling yellow-cake tales.
And the rest of us watching, shaking our heads.
And Charles Lamb trudging, heart full of faith,
to his mailbox, looking for the President's reply.

And so I asked Charles to be with us
when one of the doctors had the decency
to tell me all hope was gone. Who else
but Charles whose unwavering belief
had comforted her in happier times?
His sermons, she'd told me, started
from the earth under his feet and
lifted, and now I imagined them,
homilies walking backward
into the spiritual, homely little
scraps rising on strings to heaven.

On the day I honored Loraine's
wishes and helped her to die,
because she could not speak

for herself, Charles was there
in the hospital room and the name
of the attending nurse was Madonna.
He recited the 23rd Psalm, green
pastures, still waters, through the valley,
goodness and mercy, forever. I do not
know if Loraine heard any of it, but I hope
that she did. And he recited also from
Romans: "For I am persuaded that neither
death, nor life, not angels, nor principalities,
nor powers, not things present, nor things
to come, nor height, nor depth,
nor anything else in all creation, shall be
able to separate us from the love of God,
which is in Christ Jesus our Lord."
I do not know that Loraine heard any
of it, but hope that she did. I talked also,
and talked, standing bedside, and finally
sitting, talking, hand on her arm. I do not
know if she heard any of it, but hope she did.

Madonna said that Loraine had "passed
gracefully," and I said that I would tell
the family what she said, that it might
provide them some small comfort.
I did and it did.

It was during the shock and awe phase,
the smart bombs and guided missiles
pulverizing Iraq, or just afterward,

that I saw a photograph–we really lighted
up that night sky, didn't we? If you
didn't know what was happening
on the ground, you could have thought
it beautiful. Well, some did know,
and thought it beautiful, anyway.

The photograph: an Iraqi man, standing
in an explosion-littered street, building rubble
heaped in the background, daytime, sun shining.
His hair is as short as any middle-aged man
in America. He wears a long-sleeved shirt,
cuffs unbuttoned. He is your next door
neighbor, except that his face is turned up
to the sky, one arm lifted, fingers unclenched,
and the expression on his face, eyes squinting,
mouth open, is one of unmistakable anguish.
His is not the grief that arises from abstraction,
his country bombed, a regime changed, etc.
Someone he loved has been killed, his parents,
his children, his wife, all of them. His hand
is raised in desperate appeal, perhaps to his God,
which might, after all, be the same one as yours,
for explanation, for solace, where none will suffice.

He has a place, now, in the world, immortalized
in his grief by an embedded photographer who
has snapped the "human price of war" shot
of the day, as if there's another price that matters.
Hundreds of thousands of such photographs

could have been taken and still could, around
the globe, and should be, slammed in front
of our eyes on television, in newspapers,
magazines, on covers of Time, Newsweek,
in an unrelenting torrent until we get it.

What makes this man's arrested grief less
profound, say, than the grief of loved ones
left behind after the deaths in Oklahoma
City, after soldiers die in service to country,
to their God, less deep than your sorrow,
than mine? You thought the "Trail of Tears"
was only an interesting metaphor?

Death occurs, a biological certainty
at the end of a long life, or for a variety
of other reasons, by munitions, or whim,
disease, or ideological commitments beyond
any desire for life you can imagine. But all death
is personal. If you doubt that, there is a man in Iraq
who can vouch for it, who will tell you
where the WMD's are and who has them.
He knows and God knows.
One of these days God
will be exacting a terrible vengeance.
We will all be shaking our fists at the sky then,
our mouths full of bitter names.

Natural wood, high-beamed, arched ceiling,
and the sunlight poring through stained glass,

214

the Presbyterian chapel for Loraine's memorial
gathering, filled with family and friends , most
of the people there who loved Loraine, with whom
she'd laughed and in whose existence she'd taken
delight and, of course, the absence.

Charles Lamb is conducting the service
and he walks to the front, to behind the podium,
his face open, a slight smile. He has done this before.
He greets us, begins to speak. He says "Loraine,"
and begins to cry. Do God's eyes open wide?
God is present in this house of worship that struggled
itself into existence out of the Church of England,
right? If not here, where?
God must be present.

Charles has quickly recovered and continues.
Few may have noticed. We all sing Amazing Grace.
We have the words on sheets of paper. Wretch
like me. Ten thousand years pass in and out
of the chapel while we sing. How sweet the sound.
Friends and family take turns up front, to speak
about Loraine, tell little stories, tell about their special
relationship with her. Some I have heard. I was there.
Others I have not. They break my heart, every one.
The sunlight pulses through the stained glass. We
sing Blue Skies. I used to sing lines from that song,
the only ones I knew, when I was feeling joyful:
"Blue skies, nothing but blue skies do I see."
Now the words are "noticing the days hurrying by,"

and at the end of each verse I am saved by the swelling
voices of everyone there singing together, rising
with "Blue skies, nothing but blue skies do I see."
But I cannot imagine
I will ever sing this song again.
Outside, I never saw the sun
shining so bright, its heat shimmering
up from the parking lot.

* * *

I'm in the chair of my friend,
Sonny, the barber. We've
known one another a long time.
We went to vocational school together.
Neither of us ended up as carpenters.
Clumps of my hair fall onto my lap
and shoulders, onto the dark cloth
he has draped around me and tucked
in around my collar. I am no longer
surprised that most of it is gray.
There is a lot of it. Forgive me, Sonny.
It's been months since my last haircut.

Sonny's wife, Ann, has been dead
for three years now. Loraine and I

had gone to the funeral home to pay
our respects. It's been over a year
since Loraine's passing. Sometimes
Sonny and I look at one another
and don't say anything. Otherwise,
this is a barbershop where a lot of talk
flies around, no topic off-limits, lots
of "I gotta tell ya's," some taunting
drawing the waiting customers
into the discussions. Today there
is one other customer waiting who's
tossed a few comments into the back
and forth between Sonny and me.

I forget what the talk was that day,
but as Sonny finishes up, rubbing
tonic into my hair, the comment he makes
isn't out of left field at all, but a summary,
matter-of-fact, undeniable, beyond argument:
"God doesn't exist," Sonny says.
He furls the cloth away from me, and hair
falls to the floor. He shakes the cloth, snaps
it in the air, reaches for the push broom
"If there was a God," he says,
"Ann would still be alive."

He begins to sweep up my hair.
God knows how many hairs are on my head.
God knows how many hairs are being swept up
by the push broom. I have a vague memory

of some movie, dropped toothpicks.

I am standing up now
and the waiting customer is on his feet,
heading for the barber chair, listing
a little to one side, one hand stretched out
toward the chair as if it's a safe mooring spot.
His eyes are fixed straight ahead.
He has not said anything and the look
on his face indicates that he will not.
The smell of tonic is in the air and probably
some fine particles of hair. Sonny is sweeping,
knocking the broom against the floor, and I am
waiting for one of them to sneeze, so that I can
exclaim "God Bless You!" like a newly shorn fool.

* * *

Author's Note

For those who didn't find anything blasphemous here, I
apologize. I'll try harder next time. To those who might be
tempted to conclude, "Oh, he's just angry with God
because his wife died," I confess: that thought might have
occurred to me also if someone else had written this and I
read it. But then I would recognize the thought as

simplistic reductionism and dismiss it. I was pissed off with God long before she died. For some who may, in spite of my statement to the contrary, want to hang on to their assessment, probably because it permits them to live more securely within whatever delusion they've wrapped themselves related to God, so be it. Happy trails.

Yes, I've heard of Wounded Knee. Also read about the Crusades and the Salem witch trials and executions. God watched all of this as if it were part of a mini-series. Much of this was done, after all, in God's name. Perhaps all of this and more will be in God 2. Maybe you will write it.

This is not a history book. This is a few observations and comments related to God. You want history books, the libraries are full of them. Documents have recorded that some Japanese soldiers forcing the Bataan Death March would slip captors a handful of rice, with a quinine pill for malaria, wrapped in a banana leaf. Some militia member, one cold evening during the Trail of Tears, gave an extra blanket to an elderly woman, tossed her a chunk of corn bread. These small acts of compassion may balance the scales for you. Maybe God guided their hands.

I also know that the tribes in North America warred with one another, and committed acts of cruelty on one another, and this before Europeans showed them how to do this, and then fought with the Europeans when they arrived, raped, burned, butchered, scalped, tortured, shot with arrows, etc. So? Did pretty good for themselves having had to leap out of an essentially stone-age culture, didn't they? If that's your measure.

No, I don't hate America. Yes, I was in the military. Didn't see combat. You? Kill anybody? Did you ever, or do you now, feel you did this in service to your country? You get a pass from God on this?

Passing thought–to be angry with God is to believe God exists. You are otherwise angry with nothing. The other possibility is that you are angry with yourself for ever believing that God existed. Take your pick. You'll sort it out.

A final note: Sonny's last name is Agnello. This is Italian, which translated into English, is "lamb." Thus, Sonny being here is an ironic counterweight to Charles. It demonstrates the lengths to which God will go. Do you think that this kind of symmetry pleases God? All of this was set into motion many years ago, perhaps centuries, or even before that. There we were in Trott Vocational High School carpentry shop together, sawing a board, nailing a board, laughing, little Christs in training, never dreaming of where our lives were going or how they would intersect. God wanted me to write this and you to read it.

* * *

FOOTNOTE

Speaking of death I spoke
with Jean Lussier not long before
he died. He told me the story of his
life, of course–and how (he'd found out later)
in a small town in Quebec his mother made breakfast
and cried the morning he was to go over the Horseshoe.
He was a young man then. He was an old man when I
talked with him. He made me write it all down.
He made me copy out a long poem he'd written
about the river and God and Roger
Woodward.[1] He recited it from memory. He gave me
a minute- by-minute account of his own trip
downriver and over the falls,
what the ball did, his thoughts. He had told the story
before. Everything was in present tense.
At the end of the story, relaxed,
he settled back in his chair and said:
"I'm satisfied. Put that down, too."
So there it is.

[1] A seven year old boy who, after a boating accident (wearing only swimming trunks and a life preserver), survived a plunge over the Horseshoe Falls, 9 July, 1960.

E.R. Baxter III, Niagara County Community College Professor Emeritus of English, has been a fellow of a New York State Public Service Award for fiction and a recipient of a Just Buffalo Award for Fiction. Previous publications include *Niagara Digressions*, *Looking for Niagara*, and the chapbooks *And Other Poems*; *A Good War*; *Hunger*; and *What I Want*. Baxter is also a founding member of Niagara Heritage Partnership. (www.niagaraheritage.org)

His web site is www.erbaxteriii.com.

Photograph by Loraine L. Baxter

Abyss Publications
32 Bray Farm Road North
Yarmouthport, MA 02675-1550

Abyss Publications was founded in 1967, in a basement in Dunkirk, NY, during the mimeo revolution of Small Press Publishing, inspired by Sartre's Being and Nothingness and the notion of SUNYATA (D.T. Suzuki), combined with the winds swirling around Vladimir Mayakovsky, Samuel Beckett, W.C. Williams and Eugene Jolas. Founder: Gerard Dombrowski. Contributing Editors: Stephen Barr, Hugh Fox, Dick Higgins and Bern Porter. Abyss has persisted through relocations to Somerville and Yarmouthport, MA, embracing what the late Jonathan Williams formulated concerning Jargon Press: "The work done here can best be described by the following quotation: JARGON is not calculated to get anywhere or succeed in the American Way. It is strictly a press for maverick poets, oligarchs, characters and the most devoted of readers. One thing Olson taught us was this: "There are four legs to stand on. The first, be romantic. The second, be passionate. The third, be imaginative. And the fourth, never be rushed."

Also from Abyss Publications

Dick Higgins, *Toward the 1970's*
Dick Higgins, *Computers for the Arts*
Hugh Fox, Richard Kostelanetz, John C. Lilly, MD, and others, *After Brockman: A Symposium*
Hugh Fox, *Charles Bukowski: A Critical and Biographical Study*
Bern Porter, *89 Offenses*
Bern Porter, *The Manhattan Telephone Book*
Bern Porter, *The Wastemaker*

Gerard Dombrowski, Editor
Steve Barr, Technical Assistant
abysspublications@gmail.com

www.ingramcontent.com/pod-product-compliance
Lightning Source LLC
Chambersburg PA
CBHW051821090426
42736CB00011B/1597